WARNING

The following pages contain coarse language, sexuality, political commentary, feminism, and descriptions of emotional and sexual abuse.

Readers may find the contents of this book disturbing, triggering, and/or controversial.

Reader discretion is advised.

LOVE AND GASLIGHT

poetry by
Vironika Wilde

A publication of New Rage Poetry Press, an imprint of Soulux Press.

Cover design and chapter illustrations by Megan Faith.

ISBN: 978-1-7773516-0-1 (hardcover)
          978-1-7773516-1-8 (paperback)
          978-1-7773516-2-5 (ebook)

Poetry / Women Authors

If this story
makes you feel,
then it is for you.

Dear Vironika Tugaleva,

You wrote me a eulogy once.
I have something for you too.

Choke on it.

But only slowly.
But only purrrr.

5

SPARK

**I DON'T HATE YOU.
I HATE WHO I AM WITH YOU.**

I am a once-wild thing
jumping through hoops for snacks.

—*domesticated*

LOST LANGUAGE

"You are losing your mother tongue"
she sighs,
puts out the sour cream.

My knuckles tremble.
Step-mother,
I don't say.
You forgot your mother too.

"You must hurry up and have children soon"
she murmurs,
checks the oven.

My elbows shake.
He hurts me,
I don't say.
You disdain his breed across your table.

NOTE TO SELF #1

Just because you're always
willing to work harder
doesn't mean you should.

CREATIVE BLOCK

Sometimes, I feel
a tornado of newness
brewing in my lungs,

and I want to twist
and turn and shake
until I am a hot spiral

of voice, of hips,
of words, of laugh.
I want to scramble time.

I want to jigsaw space.
You feel my winds blow,
shiver, shut the window.

You have mastered the art
of calming the storm
I fear becoming.

ALL THINGS CONSIDERED, I'M UNDERREACTING

Every dirty dish
is a metaphor for
every loveless look
is a metaphor for
every withdrawn vow
is a metaphor for
every greedy-fingered grope
is a metaphor for
every displaced dream
is a metaphor for
every scathing outburst
is a metaphor for
every wilting wish
is a metaphor for
every way I clean up after you
is a metaphor for
every reason to leave.

CODEPENDENT'S SYNONYMOUS

The gate is open.

Even if it wasn't,
I have keys.

So why do I
stand outside,
starving and shivering,
until you ask me
to come in?

HOURGLASS

(after Randell Adjei)

I am one grain, struggling toward a tiny hole
my ultimate goal: to get to the other side
for one gasp, I am free, weightless
by the next, I am suffocating
passing time, pressed
against the glass
looking
out
there
I've seen it
real beach sand
sun-streaked, giggling
washed by the ocean waves
you say those grains are sulking
hoping they will be lucky enough to
end up in someone's windowsill timepiece
most days, I believe this—why wouldn't I—today
I am all saltwater and thirst and seagulls flying East

PROCRASTINATÌON AND PIES IN OUR SKY

I keep shielding my eyes,
waiting for you
to calm the sandstorm
but you dream windy
and pray hot air.

I keep interrupting my song,
waiting for you
to sing your part,
but you forget music
and scream silence.

I keep diverting my instincts,
waiting for you
to point the way home,
but you fake North
and drift mouth.

I keep
waiting for you
to bloom,
but you wither crux
and spore fiction.

I keep
waiting
to leave,
but.

SO ACCOMPLISHED FOR MY AGE

I rushed and rushed and
now, here I am,
standing on the edge of
nothing.

It doesn't help:
"At least I got here quickly."

It doesn't work:
"I'm not dead yet."

METICULOUS MELODRAMA

the little things   drive me crazy

I wish we were closer   I need space

sell off tenderness   buy up control

I try to warm up   but don't feel safe

you're so sweet   when I'm packing

when I close the door   you fall back in line

we are gluing feathers   the bird is long dead

nothing else hurts   like wasted time

SUNK COST BIAS

I pour my blood into all your gashes,
tell you I have more than enough.

I've called it kindness,
but it was an investment.

I never got my returns
(or your consent).

You sell me on tomorrow.
I dream of cutting my losses.

We are both gambling,
engulfed by endowment.

I am always dizzy
(but why stop now).

BIT BY BIT

I'm saving
tiny shreds of my soulfire
for you.

I'm keeping
chunks of compassion,
morsels of minutes,
flecks of holy fever,
scraps of spirit,
for you.

I'm framing
pieces of confetti promises
from you.

I'm collecting
stamps of approval,
waiting for the value to increase,
waiting for the other shoe to drop
so I can put it on and fall in line
with you.

I'm losing
portions of patience,
chunks of confidence,
fragments of faith.

I'm shedding
my trauma-twisted ties
to you.

Until all I'm left with
are tiny shards
of me.

NOTE TO SELF #2

You're allowed
to feel a desperate desire
to experience life again
and to follow that desire
wherever it beckons.

USSR COLLECTIVE FARMS

"The men spent all day drinking"
she tells me,
"while the women did all the work."

I have never.

"The women worked all day"
she tells me,
"and then they cooked and cleaned too."

I have never been one.

"The women cooked and cleaned"
she tells me,
"and then took care of the children."

I have never been one to miss.

"The women took care of the children"
she tells me,
"and then took care of the men."

I have never been one to miss a metaphor.

MIRROR IMAGE MISERY

I am sick with
my own self-judgment
masquerading as my assumptions
about other people's judgments of me.

COMMON, CRUCIAL, AND RARE

I keep watering the weeds
    that throttle the rarest
        flowers in my garden.

A reformed weed myself,
    how could I ever prune?
        The crime of hypocrisy.

Ever the extremist, I feed
    that which drains me, then
        I wonder why I'm so tired.

I broke today, smiled at
    the milky blood and soil
        on my palms, guiltless.

It's not that Common deserves
    to die—I pull, sigh—it's that
        Rare needs room to root.

SENTIENT HAZARD

A few beers in, one, two,
you spill what you call
the truth. It corrodes
everything in its path:
cemented promises,
budding tenderness.

A few beers in, three,
four, you billow smoke
through a scowl. I choke
on the fumes. Real love,
you spit, would uncover
her face.

A few beers in, five,
six, you ooze insight
turned caustic under
pressure. You call me
the catalyst. I believe it.
I try. I alter my structure.
It changes nothing.

(One day, I read that
a real catalyst causes
a reaction, but remains
the same. And you,
my dear, never change.)

LEARNING TO COOK

I catch a whiff of your
delicious expectations.

How easy it would be
to swallow them whole.

I let myself nibble on
your version of reality,

but I never feel nourished
after these empty pleasures.

Your approval is my treat.
My own is my dinner.

WHAT I'VE LEARNED (APPARENTLY)

how to wander a madhouse corridor at dawn

when the sheets turn to trenches, sleep on the couch

10K keeps the doubts away

ice cubes under your eyes reduce signs of crying

what a safe space isn't

obsessive cleaning helps avoid facing soul scum

24K keeps the doubts away

how to work in a prison as cook, cleaner, guard,
treasurer, nurse—everything but warden

where to cache the lists and spirals

when everyone says they can't even imagine him
getting angry, look at her eyes

TALE AS OLD AS TIME

She was a girl
who couldn't grasp
how beautiful she was,
and he didn't want her to
because he was afraid
of the competition.

—He says "I love you" but means "Don't leave me"

UNCRITICAL GRACE

the spiritual book is a byproduct of fear
toes skimming the crater / gurus talk deep

the creative impulse is a byproduct of fear
the cavern sighs, coaxes / art resists

the love of our lives is a byproduct of fear
we smile in death's face as s/he looms

the act of courage is a byproduct of fear
fearlessness is an act / be afraid, be brave

MIRROR VOWS

One day, no one will
call me young or new.
No one will say, "You still have
your whole life ahead of you."

When my deathbed is
close enough to smell,
will my fingers be sticky,
lips smirking farewell?

Or will I stare blankly
at a clean, empty plate,
having waited politely,
and now it's too late?

I can't betray her again,
this someday reflection.
I can't afford to pretend
those eyes had no questions.

I'll let them shine brightly,
blaze my way through the dark.
Dear spirit, do you hear me?
I *will* protect your spark.

IF THIS IS ENLIGHTENMENT, I DON'T WANT IT

Trying to right the wrongs of my past
by being a "good person"
has suffocated me more
than the abuse that led me to those wrongs
in the first place.

NOT EVEN THE SAME BOOKSHELF

We dug and dug and now,
now that we've unearthed
this chasm between us,
we stand here silently,
wondering whether this is
an exercise in acceptance
or a test of self-respect.

NOTE TO SELF #3

You'll never know
who you are
unless you shed
who you pretend to be.

HAVING KIDS

It's not like I'm against procreation.

If you and I were so obsessed with each other
that we couldn't help but spawn—
how could it feel wrong?

But we aren't. Let's be honest.

I have no urge
to personify our dysfunction.

THINGS I SAID TO YOU

I can't be myself around you. I have trust issues.

I must be on the Autism spectrum because when you hold my hand, I feel like I'm suffocating under something heavy and can't take a full breath until I get out.

I feel like a lampshade.

I don't miss you when you're gone, but I don't miss anything. Maybe I'm just really mindful. Maybe you should try it.

I can't be myself around you. I don't trust you.

I don't like it when anyone touches me there. Or there. Ugh, especially there. I must have low sexual desire. I'll read a book about it. I'll try to fix it for us: my lack of interest.

I feel like a war wife.

The sound of you eating is repulsive to me. I think I have misophonia. Yeah, that's a real thing. It's been linked to creative genius, you know.

I can't be myself around you. I need to trust myself on this.

I feel. I can't. I need.

I.

WHY?

We both knew
something wasn't quite right,
but we clung on,
used each other like cigarettes:
casual, habitual, slow death.

Why?

I STAY: ALTERNATE ENDING SUMMARY

We are diagonal:
either plummeting to our quarterly rock bottom
or renewing our yearly subscription to hope.

We take shallow gasps:
you clutch your lungs to hush raging blood,
I clench my throat to hush warning screams.

We call it love:
tomorrow promises an antidote for today's poison,
today looks at yesterday with arrogant eyes.

We are each other's answers to simple questions.

We have a pine box to call home.

GREENER PASTURES

Where will we graze now,
if not on one another's fields
of shared mediocrity?

"WHY DIDN'T YOU LEAVE SOONER?"

He smeared tar on my wings.
Use gasoline, they said. Use kerosene.
I didn't trust myself flammable and fire-tongued.

He built a cage to shelter me.
Forget the sky, he said. Forget flying.
I chose the hunter in my bed over those in the bush.

He cherished my beak, my tail, my chirp.
I can't sing for you, I said. I can't even inhale.
I gulped gas, burned Phoenix, flew away belting.

I didn't leave. I died. I was reborn.
Why didn't I resurrect sooner, you ask?
Because miracles take time.

4

HEAT

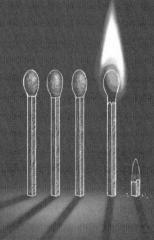

NOTE TO SELF #4

Stop regretting and idealizing past lovers.
There's a reason you left.
You keep missing comfort, missing home,
but what if what you're missing
are feelings you haven't had yet—
feelings you daydreamed about
before you lowered your standards?

MIDNIGHT VOLCANO

I don't remember when the Earth shook. Maybe I was underwater. Maybe we made magma. Maybe our breaths converged mid-stanza. It all happened so quickly, and now, three thousand miles away, I'm still erupting. I'm oozing with words that block out the sun, sending smoke signals to you. Lava drips from my lips. My heart seeps ashes. Some have plunged into my molten rivers, turned obsidian, and in just the right light, you can still see the fossilized plead around my sneer. This is a travel advisory. Exercise a high degree of caution. I overflow with red-hot omens that cool into bitter, basalt myths. Be ready. Be brave. And don't come back when the sky is clear, my crater cold and hollow, tell me you needed time. It's now or never. It's real or it's not.

MUSE

You are a warrior,
a hunter,
a labyrinth,
a Buddha,
a reminder to anyone who doubts it that
the human spirit is a fumbling enigma and
bleeding art is the only way to survive this ride.

The universe trickles prophecies through your fingers.
The cosmos drizzles scriptures through your mouth.

You Bart Simpson.
You Janis Joplin.
You Mozart.
You Shakti.
You sunrise.
You sunset.

You soft-petalled, prismatic pandemonium.
You cold-pressed, mischievous catharsis.

You are the closest thing
in this world to heaven,
and if I had to die to touch you,
even for a moment, I would.

You ignite all that is cryptic and holy inside me,
and I can almost taste the stars when you smile.

YIN YANGS OF TRASH AND STARDUST

You are the rock
that roots my fire.
You are the earth
that grounds my soul.

OR

It happens often. More often than you know. Like when you made me a flower out of the paper scraps I felt guilty throwing away. Like when we sustain eye contact and your pupils start sparkling. Like when you inch closer, brush against me, and I want to fall deep, deep down into you (or want you to fall deep, deep down into me). But. I am afraid of how I fall. But. I don't know how to come back to the ground after diving into the ocean. So. I keep falling silently. In my head. In my hips. And I want you to notice. Or.

YOU, ME, AND ART

It might have been when
I said, "I feel like we're
in a threesome with you, me, and art."
You said, "That's so hot."

It might have been when
you said, "God, art, beauty, love, truth—
is there really a difference between these things?"
I answered, "No."

I don't know when
I began to forget the difference

between rereading a poem for the twentieth time
and being awestruck by the delicacy of a flower

between saying, "I love you"
and saying, "I believe in a unified creative force"

between caressing your neck
and making a fine line with my paintbrush

between the rhythm that pours out of my flesh
and nights when we're both tired but can't keep still.

God is in every room with us,
and she wants more.

EXQUISITELY CRAFTED NOSTALGIA

Poetry craves a good mystery
standby
a narrative with unclear boundaries
rolling
a novel with an unpredictable ending
action
fictional struggle and made up triumphs
close-up
I fear the words running dry
long shot
I run back to where I've died
crossfade
I expect a different plotline
tilt
you're an actor in a manuscript I write
dissolve
you stay on script, line by line
pan
you audition so well every time
fade
this could be so right
cut
if it wasn't only in my mind
wrap

ADVICE FROM A THERAPY STUDENT

You seem like
the kind of person
who spends a lot of time
with people who
are dangerous
for you.

Your standards for
a good relationship
are lower than you realize.

You think these things
are so wonderful to find
in a person, but they're basic.

Feeling safe is a basic thing.

LEARN TO PLAY

my beautiful   guitar

collects dust   in the corner

gentle neck   supple frame

unplucked strings   such craftsmanship

I don't take time   to learn to play

but I keep it   just in case

please don't   do that to me

WINTER

I can't even touch myself.
I haven't washed the sheets.
As I wander the streets,
the wind howls in my face.
A blanket grows over my shoulders,
curls around my ankles.

I stop dancing, devour sentences.
February freezes me inside out.
Gusts ignite the embers;
crimson remnants of our bonfire.
I will not comb the woods for kindling.
I'm pining for the fuel that erupts
when my lips linger on your neck.

It must be easier for you.
You don't eat fire for breakfast.
This blanket is heavy, comfortable.
The air grows colder, impossible
to get up, save the dwindling coals.

It's okay to cry. I say this out loud.
I squeeze my arms tightly, tighter.
I light candles, burn incense.
I take out the recycling.

I still can't wash the sheets.
Your face is the first thing I see
when I wake up to these pillows,
but I won't forget the difference
between surrender
and giving up.

GOSSIP

I overhear the neighbour
on the phone. He says,
"Well, she is a poet, you know."

He lowers his voice.
I don't hear the rest,
but it's comforting.

Whatever he is praising
or complaining about
can be humanized
by my art.

SORRY, I'VE BEEN VERY BUSY LATELY

air
The barista asks me how I am. Forget I'm-fine-thanks-how-are-you, I say, "I'm trying to fight falling into the void." She says she understands, passes me the debit machine. How did I get here?

water
Music makes it worse. I should make a metaphor. I can't find one. This isn't writing. It's 3:31 am. I walk to the lake, slide around on thick ice like a figure skater, stomp around on thin ice like a giant. Soaking my boots makes me laugh. A fork in the road makes me cry. I wake up hoping it's over.

fire
The sunshine hurts my retinas. I want to disappear. I want to reappear. I brainstorm solutions: drink benzene, snort glass, chew cement, slurp air, smoke plastic, burn my eyelashes off one by one by one, mix the ashes with strychnine, gobble it down.

earth
I refuse. No. So what if I can't cry? No. I'm not 23 anymore. I WILL NOT HURT MYSELF JUST TO FEEL ALIVE.

space
Yes. I close my eyes. Catch me. I won't look down. Catch me. I'm flying now. Catch me. Forget these scars and regrets. Love me, great, wide void. Love me like I deserve.

NOTE TO SELF #5

If you need to
cut off parts of yourself,
it is not real love,
and it will not work.
Do you hear me?
It won't work.

MY NEW BODYGUARD

You tell me your tongue needs my mouth.
You tell me there's a cot upstairs.

You sing to me, whisper in my ear.
Offerings to the Goddess, and she

is almost pleased. She wants to know
if you will solve the riddles in me

after you satiate your loneliness.
Smile on her face, laughing eyes.

She inquires if you will respect me,
honour me, admire me, as much as

I have you. Her hand on my shoulder.
I'm quivering, begging to be released

to you. She says it's for my own good.
You've got to take this up with her now.

LATE TO WORK BECAUSE OF THE JUMPER

It must be nice
not to understand why
he couldn't have done it quietly
and not bothered anybody.

LEAVING

You say it's not because you
don't like me that you're leaving.

Why *are* you leaving?
Are *you* leaving?

Leaving is such a verb
in a world full of nouns,

bold and self-assured
and dripping in silver.

I spend every penny
to afford more of it

while one day intending
to sell it all (with interest)

for someone to love.

HOW TO BREAK A HEART IN 7 EASY STEPS

1. Spot her. You know the one. She smiles all tough, but her eyes call home on a rainy Sunday afternoon, and no one answers.

2. When she opens the gates, enter boldly. Sample the trust she aged carefully in the cellar. Tell her you are a connoisseur of beauty.

3. Take and take until her supernova turns black hole. Until she can't taste morning anymore and asks you to remind her. Don't. Don't you dare walk through her portals when she says the fridge is empty and the cellar is dry.

4. Give fear the keys. Sit in the passenger seat.

5. Close your eyes. Do not look in the rear-view.

6. Do not wonder how she is.

7. Assume you've done no harm.

STILL HERE

You're gone now, but

I am still here
high on renegade recollections, invisible illusions,
correcting spelling mistakes in our slush pile fiction.

I am still here
though I wake up ravenous for cold lang syne,
bleeding from the shrapnel of our swan song.

I am still here
snivelling over feathers and splashes of yellow,
adjusting my sails to navigate your wake.

I am still here
cleaning the crimson guillotine after its final chop,
laying flowers on the gravestone of my reborn purity.

I am still here
drowning sheep, itching to name this a nightmare,
disembowelling devotion, wailing what went wrong.

I am still here
but here isn't the same place without you.

I am still here
waiting for you to come back.

MASTER OF THE HOUSE

He tangles his fingers,
ready to wage war,
says he wants to be
proven wrong for once.
He's open to being wrong.
He really is.

He wears a crown
studded with diamond lies.
He was heartbroken
when I stopped loving him
the way only a little girl
with no concept of
right and wrong can love.

He is everywhere.
The past is a house of mirrors
I long to escape,
but everywhere I turn,
I see the same face.
Someone has to sit in that chair
and put on Master's crown.

If you offered me belonging
that doesn't creak or crumble
under the weight of all my hungers,
I would run first, wonder why later.

When there's no one to mistreat me,
I don't know how to be in love.

CHASING SHADOWS

I miss you like the Dry Valleys in Antarctica
miss the snow
as in
it never snows there.

I miss you like the Atacama desert
misses the rain
as in
it never rains there.

I miss you the way you used to
miss me
as in
you never did.

I miss the way the point
misses me
as in
I never learn.

NEW RAGE

We are on the floor of the sage and crystal house.
I'm afraid to ask her when I'll be able to move in.

She's gyrating on the carpet, moaning, tells me
she took a microdose. Her pupils are blueberries.

"I'm full of hatred," I say. "It scares me.
I'm full of anger and despair. I want it to stop."

She trembles. Her eyeballs roll. She says,
"You created this. You the universe created this."

I raise my voice, hiss, "I did not create *him*."
Churning fury to tears is an avoidant habit.

"But you did, love," she coos. "You wanted
to experience this. You wrote this story."

"I hate him," I whisper, "I don't want to.
It's embarrassing. But I hate him." Sniff.

She smirks, undulates. "You created him.
You chose him, like you chose your parents."

I nod, wipe my cheeks, tell her I understand,
skip town, and boycott the New Age movement.

The revived wolf growls. The fearful woman cries.
But how easy it once was: the coveted Right Thing.

SCAREDY CAT

slither

His name is Worm. His owner tells me I'll understand why once I see how he slithers. She says he must not know what a hiss means. He runs out of every room I enter. His tail is broken in half. Worm is a caterpillar, petrified of the cocoon after some excited child trapped him in a glass jar. He hisses at me as I fill his bowl. I tell him I understand. And I do.

sneak

His eyes are curious. He sniffs my hand, flinches. That night, I catch him on top of the couch looking defeated. I reach out. He doesn't move. It's the first time I stroke his fur. His neck is tense. His eyes are sad. I tell him it's okay. I don't tell him I won't hurt him because I'm not in control of his pain. After I take my hand away, he looks both relieved and desperate for more. I tell him I don't know how to feel safe either.

crawl

He jumps out of bed to avoid me. I follow him. I get on my knees and say, "I'm not who hurt you." His mouth is open mid-hiss. His stare punctures my tear ducts. I say, "I'm not the one who hurt you, but it still hurts, and you can't forget." He blinks, closes his mouth. His expression is pathetic, intense, sad, like a 9-year-old girl. I say, "I can't forget either." He walks away when I start sobbing, goes to his food bowl. My forehead hits the floor. We are alone in the nightmare worlds we carry around—full of past, full of fear. I slither back into bed, hoping he'll follow me. He doesn't. I tell him I understand. And I do.

squirm

His owner says he hisses much less now. I send her a list of tips about his behaviour. Don't give food right after he hisses; wait ten seconds or until he meows. Give bits of food while petting him to pair safety with human touch. Be patient. Don't try to do too much at once. Let it happen slowly. And I wonder if I should make a list for future lovers. Don't reach out right after I pull away; wait a few days or until I say "Please" or "I'm scared" or "This is hard for me, you know." Tell me the truth as you hug me (to pair safety with human touch). Be patient. Don't try to do too much at once. Let it happen slowly. And if you are not ready to treasure a creature who cannot forget, do not take me into the warmth of your arms. You will only make it worse.

writhe

When I come to visit, Worm stays under the bed. I tell him I understand. As I leave, I wonder if he smelled me. Mostly, I wonder which opportunities come to visit while I hide inside my memories. I catch my glance in a bathroom window. I tell her I want more. I tell her I deserve better. And I do.

NOTE TO SELF #6

Most of your healing journey
will be about unlearning
the patterns of self-protection
that once kept you safe.

LUCKY YOU

I should be happy for you.

You've sidestepped my evolution
from Goddess to grievance.

That crazy ex-girlfriend you once had.
That wild chick you fucked once.
That bitch you no longer talk to.

Congratulations on escaping me.

You would have hook-line-sunk
into me ignoring all your flaws.
I would have grown bored with it,
raised the bar, choked on your scent.

Dodged that bullet. Lucky you.

THE LONELY VIRUS

Loneliness is a disease
spread by people who
try to use other people
to cure their loneliness.

—*Satisfying a craving doesn't heal the addiction*

HOLD ON

I want to be held, and the things that hold me down do half a job. Some days, I can't even fix it. Some days, I rot on the inside and refuse to cut myself down. Some days, my fruits hit pavement, explode with seeds meant for soil, and only *I* understand what a wreckage my smile is. Joy is a weight. It's heavy. Can't you carry it for me while I tread around entropy, run my nails down its spine? Put one hand on each hip, square your shoulders, grip tightly. The future is trying to take me. Hold me back. Hold me down. Hold on until you're done. Ignore me as you reach for your pants. You knew all along, didn't you? A blindfold knows its job. At the end of the day, the most selfish thing is trying to help another person.

A LOVE STORY ALONE

I'm afraid.
I'm afraid to be myself.
I'm afraid of being too much.
I'm afraid I'm not beautiful,
and there's nothing in me worth seeing
except your own reflection.

So, let me love you.

Let me love you like I can't love myself.
Let me love your flaws like I can't love mine.
Let me shower you with this gold
I don't feel worthy of carrying in my hips.

Let me smile at your fears:
so tame and sweet compared to mine,
until I feel your pain after you're gone,
absorb your trauma, your family's trauma.

Let me tie your pain around my neck,
keeping one hand over my trachea
and one hand over your heart
as I carry us *both* into tomorrow.

Let me prostrate by the foot of this pedestal I
constructed for you, waiting for a snack of approval
to hold me over until you're not too busy anymore.

Let me bury my voice, water it every day
with casual acts of self-loathing,
so I can build you a beanstalk
to the heavens of your dreams.

Let me dance to the rhythm of your metronome,
so I don't have to worry about
singing my own melody off-key.

Let me get lost in your eyes
without a map or compass,
pass out under your arctic sky,
wake up with frostbite, and then
write a poem about the patterns in my necrotic skin.

Let me help you build your legacy
while quietly building mine on the side,
pick up the chores if you're in for a ride with the
voices in your head, but when it's my turn, let me
do you the favour of battling my demons alone
because you don't know how to hold
the woman who holds you.

So, let me love you...
until we *both* get sick of you,
until we *both* can't stomach
your pseudomedicine, your empty words.

Until I take my love back,
the same love I don't give myself
when I wake up feeling like there's no reason to live
and anyone I talk to says things that don't help,
can't help; and I will never admit I need help.
I keep making beauty out of the pain,
so no one sees how insane I can be when I'm alone.

And I've taken refuge in your skin
to escape the scars and cellulite on mine
too many times, and now
the skin I keep taking off and putting back on
is getting stretched out, worn out,
and I don't know how to feel held
in an identity I keep revising
every time I think someone might show me
what home feels like.

I write these epic romances
that wither into tragedies when—surprise!—
the person I stamped as my safe space

turns out to be a ball and chain
around everything truly worthwhile in me.

I've been running from myself my whole life.

Even my ideas about self-love,
I've dressed up in their Sunday best.

Real self-love means owning that, sometimes,
I feel like the universe sees me as a mistake
it tries to correct through my sleepless thoughts.

Real self-love means owning that
the tough times make art too,
so I have to watch what I mean when I say
that I'm an artist following my creative energy
wherever it takes me because sometimes it takes me
to the edge of a cliff miles away from anyone else
and, in those moments, it doesn't matter how many
pretty stories I've written about other people.
It only matters that I haven't written any about me.

I have to own that the strength people keep
seeing in me comes from holding on when
every single cell in my body wants to eject
out of this existence in hopes that
there's somewhere more welcoming
to live in this universe
than the inside of my head.

I have to own that, call it mine,
like when we go camping
and someone asks whose garbage it is.

It's mine.

And I can't help clean anything else up right now
because there's so much here.
There's no garbage can big enough
for the trash in my head.

It's mine:
this imagination steering me into the abyss
because it wants to go on a joyride.

It's mine.

It is probably going to be too much for you.

But maybe this sword I keep
cutting myself trying to wield
is meant for greater things than
knighting the men who share my bed.

Maybe my soul is too high voltage for romance.

Maybe my words are meant to
power thousands of hearts
but I keep electrocuting myself
and everybody who gets close to me
because I'm afraid to be myself,
afraid of being too much.
afraid that I'm not beautiful.

So.

I'm going to take all this "love" I keep giving away
and bathe my fears in it for a little while.

Maybe real self-love
starts with
being happy alone.

WE DID IT TOGETHER

I gathered the bones I called ugly.
You came to help me sing them dead.
It almost looked like love.

THE KING WHO FEELS NOTHING

That cold familiar sting of strung-out tire swings.

That catastrophic ache of his catatonic chaos
never failed to make a woman jealous.

That infinity-void-infinity of the diamonds in his eyes
got used to seeing a poet cry.

That breathless biting bullet of words no longer true
found a fairy tale perfect to connect with you.

That lonely-never-aloneness of fire without warmth
looks like a cozy haven to a stray who self-harms.

That butterfly so brave (but of course it's not forever)
traps salt inside the cut, wonders what's the matter.

That so familiar act-end-scene
of what could have never been.

That old-same, same-old thing
of throneless queens and kings.

That swing, tire(d), swing.

That I gave you everything.

That *ring*.

That is the final thing.

ENOUGH

I have had enough of
half-wanting half-love,
half-perfect half-words.

I don't need anyone to
put me on a pedestal.

I'll climb up there myself,
cloak symbols in the breeze.

My words carry my essence
like carrier pigeons,
like telegrams,
like all the songs
you never wrote me.

My poems enliven my vigour
like waterfalls,
like whirlwinds,
like all the places
you never touched me.

I had to lose you
to understand that.

I had to lose you
to find me again.

NOTE TO SELF #7

Stop.

Stop wandering back to the border
of a country that never cared
to give you asylum or shelter.

Stop wandering back to the embrace
of a creature who never wanted
to hold you tightly or for long.

Stop wandering back to the silence
of a mouth that never wanted
to hear you speak or answer.

Stop wandering back to the end
of the last poem you never wrote
to The One who isn't or won't.

Stop wondering if it was real,
if he couldn't or wouldn't try.

He didn't.

That's all you need to know.

Stop, babe.

Beautiful girl, STOP.

3

FIRE

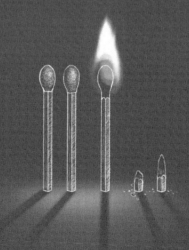

WANT ME? EAT THE VOICES IN MY HEAD.

Fuck me.
I mean, do it how I like it.
I mean, respect me.
I mean, why don't you ever listen?
I mean, why is it so hard to be myself around you?
I mean, who let you decide who I get to be?
I mean, I think it was me.
I mean, I forgot myself in your skin.
I mean, it's hard to live in mine.
I mean, sometimes it's lonely.
I mean, I am some kind of crazy.
I mean, save me.
I mean, fuck me.

THE BEATEN PATH TO A MAN'S HEART

"Girls in my village…"

When I say Boy has been cooking for himself,
she gasps, says I must cook for him or lose him.
Months later, Boy loses me.

"…were only considered marriage material…"

When I say Man can spoon his own food,
she frowns, says I must serve him or lose him.
Years later, Man loses me.

"…if they could cook a different soup…"

When I say Old Man should eat what he wants,
she grimaces, says I shouldn't pity a deadweight.
Decades later, she cannot lose him.

"…for every day of the year."

RED FLAGS

When he has an empty refrigerator,
says he wants to get some food,
orders a beer before the waitress
opens her mouth to say, "Hello."

When his refrigerator is full of food
his mother bought for him.

When he makes jokes at the waitress,
keeps vying for her attention in front of you.

When his bookshelf contains
titles like *The Layguide* and
his vocabulary includes
terms like "last-minute resistance."

When you ask him
how he would spend his time
if he had only one year left to live,
his answer doesn't mention you,
and he doesn't ask you
the same question back.

When he wants you more than you want him.

When you want him more than he wants you.

When he hates his mother.
Especially if you hate your father.

When he hates his mother
and you hate your father
but neither of you admits it
because "hate is wrong" and
you're bypassing all the pain.

When he says he wants a family,
pulls out when he's about to cum
like he's holding a blowtorch,
saving you both from burns.

When you finish yourself off after he leaves.

When you finish yourself off while he's still there.

When you don't finish for weeks,
and he doesn't consider this
as a potential explanation to why
you're so emotional all the time.

When he tells you he's afraid of hurting you.

When he tells you he's not going to hurt you.

When kissing him feels like
something is being stolen from you.

When you change who you say you are
to create space for who you've had to become
to make room for all his insecurities.

When you have any doubt whatsoever
about singing or dancing in front of him
or being honest about how you feel
or asking for what you want.

When he acts like a victim
after he empathizes with you.

When you feel like a victim
after empathizing with him.

When all his Gods are male,
and the women he deifies
are Madonnas, virgins, "pure."

When all your poems are about him,
but none of his songs are about you.

When the red flags don't matter,
even when you notice them on the spot.

When the most important thing
is the poetry that flows out of you
around him, even when the poems
are depressing, angry, self-loathing.

When nothing matters more than
being wrapped in his arms, but
he doesn't know how to touch you.

When he keeps telling you that
he doesn't miss you, doesn't need you,
can't marry you, won't stick around,
and you pride yourself on how patient
you're being with all his anxieties.

When he says he's giving you space
every time you need him,
says he's leaving out of love.

When you believe this is love.

SONG AS OLD AS RHYME

Your pleasure lived
one inch North of his,
so you moved into
his daydream of you
and started faking home.

—*Agitation is her dissent; ennui is her strike*

LOVING WITHOUT ATTACHMENT

Love without attachment,
the spiritual traditions say,
but who wrote these rules?
I doubt women were involved.

Stay cold, distant, detached,
the spiritual traditions say,
but whom do you abandon
when you go wandering
into your noiseless attic?

And is one of those remains
a part of you that is a little
too human for your liking?

You push away desires
like they are diseases
while purifying yourself of
all that is of the flesh.

And you don't even understand
how disgustingly prejudiced
it all is, or how exclusive.

NOTE TO SELF #8

Never, ever stop feeling.
Do not go numb.
The world, even with all its horror,
is too beautiful to miss.

"I'LL LET IT SLIDE JUST THIS ONCE, SWEETHEART."

He smiles ear to ear,
tells me he's going to help me
this one time.

(And thank goodness
he was here to rescue me
out of the quicksand
he shoved me into.)

That same-cold
Prince Charming bullshit.

We both know that
his family owns this tower
and the dragon takes bribes.

HALF-WOMAN, HALF-KALEIDOSCOPE

1   I was a woman with a jet plane. You wanted to fly in a rocket ship. I loaned you my keys, trusted. I flew you up into the stratosphere, cheered. And you? You always left the gas tank empty.

2   In the bathroom of the refuel station, I found gospel, naked and misspelled, ignored by all the women too busy regaining strength for their every-day Olympics.

3   I gave up my jet plane, picked up a pen, wrote all the things I didn't say to you: that when I looked closely at your hands for the first time, I knew they would never hold all my galaxies; that I was half-woman, half-kaleidoscope—always changing, rearranging—and you were not ready for my art; that it took surgery (hours, forceps, blood) to remove your judgment from my spine, stand up tall again, and I'm still afraid of giving too much.

4   I looked down at my words, ashamed. Why tell the tale of yet another well full of garbage, begging to be cleaned, while the whole town drinks bottled water? Don't we already know? Isn't that why we got in those jet planes, learned to fly? So we could leave those wells behind, forget?

5   Oh, how we have tried to forget. Each time we asked for a Polo to our Marco, they've run away, so we learned not to ask. Each time we tore open our pelvises to purge the demons haunting our wombs, they've told us to stop being dramatic, so we learned not to purge. We tried to forget how the

famished innocence we keep bundled in tattered, bloodstained blankets is tired of foster care.

6   We tried to forget. We tried to crawl back into the space between the two ribs they say we came from, but we're too big now. And what if we always were? What if that rib was a sacrifice to the Goddess, who in turn sent her own messenger with its own moral: the snake that convinced us to bite the delicious truth and lose our ignorance, whatever the price—where is that part of the story?

7   Where's the part about Eve being shamed and blamed for reaching into the macrocosm of knowledge, hating herself for eons before realizing that even if the best-selling book of all time calls her a traitor and a witch, she was still right? That she'd bite that apple again if she had the chance?

8   When will we accept that we have always been gatekeepers to the multiverse—full of sun and moon, full of sky and ocean floor, full of honey and arsenic—and that there are lessons in our so-called hysteria, our drama, our inconvenient turns of mood?

9   I searched and searched the graffiti at those refuel stations, looking for answers. I found nothing, but not because nothing had been written. Erasure is the job of the bathroom attendant who's sick of his wife's nagging.

10   No matter how many boys have run from me as I spilled prophecy from my chapped, sore lips, soaked in question marks, it was still true. It was true even when I did not believe it.

11   Until we build spaceships, aim them at the great, wide cosmos, reaching for the apples in the sky together, until we clean the unwritten history books out of our wells and fill our bellies with fresh, cold respect, I'm staying in the dirt with my pen.

12   Change has come. Tell me, can you smell it? Tell me, when my sisters beckon you with the bright, red truth that holds every poisonous lie in its center, will you take a bite? Will you let our blood spill over your clean, white sheets and, in the end, say thank you? (Thank you for being allowed to witness the universe knowing itself.) Or will you tell us to go clean ourselves up?

13   It's still your choice. It always has been. The difference is we're paying attention now. Do what you want, but know this: your choices will be judged.

WHO PUT THE SHAM IN SHAMANIC?

In the Wrong Part of Town, it's a curse.
Here, we have half-baked traditions
from a culture we neither belong to
nor give back to; here, it's medicine.
Here, drink up.

ASKING FOR IT

I sit naked in the sun.
The flies land on me.
I brush them away.
Who can relax like this?

They land on me again.
How can I enjoy myself?

They come for my thighs,
my nipples, everything
exposed. I go inside.

Flies will be flies.
What is there to do?

TO THE DAUGHTER I MIGHT NEVER HAVE

When you hear
something nasty about
one of your sisters,
even if it is
a comment from her own lips,
don't repeat it out loud.

Do not furnish fear.

When you hear
something kind about
one of your sisters,
especially if it is
a thought in your head,
tell her twice.

Do not hoard kindness.

When you fall for
one of the boys
who flip through girls
like cards in a Rolodex,
looking for one who is
less crazy than the others,
don't pretend to be one.

Do not negotiate dignity.

Run.

WHEN WOMEN DISAPPEAR

Cinderella lived happily ever after
as in
nobody's heard from her since
as in
shouldn't we go check on her?

#METOO

Some say it's only rape if you say "No,"
but "No" was another language—
a foreign tongue I never learned.

As a young girl, I didn't know
the difference between being
used and being loved. (I am
not sure I know it now.)

Who is responsible:
The men who don't hear the "No,"
or the girl who doesn't say it?
However you answer
the question, it does not
erase the scars.

BYPASSANA

When the sky rains blood and bile,
and your face remains unblemished,
don't call this inner peace.

When the world becomes a rockfall,
and your mind stays clear as a lake,
don't call this enlightenment.

When the arid earth cries for rainfall,
and your eyes stay dry as deserts,
don't call this love or light.

NOTE TO SELF #9

You do not need any more strength.
You need to realize how strong you already are.

WHAT MAKES A WOMAN

She says,
"You don't know
how many bills I have paid
with these tits."

For a wild moment,
I recall my pile of bills
and wonder
what makes a real woman.

MEN

1. We meet in a chat room. His screen name has the word "angel" in it. I'm in elementary school. His age ends in a 6. Is it 26? 36? 46? I don't remember. I remember his beard. It's my first kiss. I never see him again.

2. We meet outside the Walmart where I'm selling chocolates. I am 11. He's twice my height. He tells me he lives in a castle, asks to grab my breasts, doesn't wait for an answer. I don't tell him to stop. His friend looks uncomfortable, mumbles something about me being underage. When my boss picks me up, he shouts, "Why did you let him touch you? Why?! Don't let people do this." No one tells my parents.

3. We meet in a chat room, arrange to meet at Kipling station. He tells me my face is a 6 and my body is a 9. I take it as a compliment.

4. He goes to my school, adds me on Messenger, calls me on the phone, tells me my voice doesn't match my body. He's on the football team. He ignores me in front of his friends.

5. We meet on campus. I use the gym but I'm not a student. I'm entering high school. He's 23. He convinces me to go down on him in the bathroom stall. For weeks, I wait for him to call like Cinderella waited to try on the glass slipper. He doesn't. I tell a friend. Her mom prohibits her from talking to me, says, "Can't be friends with a girl like that."

6. He says, "Parents should be able to sexually educate their children." She frowns, grumbles some dissent. He snaps, "Don't pretend you wouldn't do it." His hands are innocent, but I can't forget what happened in his head.

7. I don't tell him I'm a virgin. We smoke something. I don't remember if he smokes it too. I go to La La Land. He carries me up a hill because I can't walk, puts me paralyzed onto his floor, plays "Youth of the Nation" over and over, and has no idea that he's my first ...or does he?

8. His idea of foreplay is jamming his fingers in and out of me as quickly as he possibly can. We break a lot of condoms because I'm too dry. He tells me girls can't climax sometimes, and that's how it is. He says he learned this in health class.

9. I call him the love of my life. I wake up to the stench of whiskey. He's huffing and puffing on top of me. I stare into the corner, inventing symmetries in spider webs. We don't talk about it. It happens again.

10. We meet in a club, go out back. There's a dumpster involved. Are we on top of it? Against it? Behind it? It's blurry. He hands me $20 without making eye contact. I take it, cry in the cab, pay with the bill.

11. He's a club bouncer, gives me lines of cocaine while clutching my waist, my back, my thigh, never too far. We do this every week.

12. He is my roommate's family friend. I look up at him while he's inside me and think, "Wow, you're having a really good time, aren't you?" I go celibate.

13. I call him my partner. He hates feminists. I tell him I want our first time to be special. The moment I let my guard down, he barges in. That night, I don't sleep. Six months after we break up, he says he doesn't remember our first time because he was too drunk, says he's sorry. Six months before we break up, I tell him I'm afraid of never experiencing myself fully. He says he's afraid of never having better sex.

14. I call him my soul mate. He reminds me of my dad. I trust him so much, I'd let him do anything to me. He says he doesn't know what I mean by that. More often than not, he rolls over and falls asleep while I stay up, thoughts racing, tissues burning, confused. I tell my friends it's the best sex I've ever had. It's not a lie.

15. He's a spiritual healer, a Tantric masseuse, or so he says. He says he can fix me. I let him try. It's not until months later, when he starts preying on my friends, that I start calling it what it was.

16. He listens. He wants to decipher me. His pleasure comes not from using me but from bringing me to ecstasy. He... is a fantasy. He... might be a She. She... is a fantasy. I write, "Am I asking for too much?" I delete it and write, "I'm not asking for that much." I delete it and write, "I'm not settling for less." I delete it and write, "Could this be real?" I delete it. I want to delete this whole poem. I don't.

THE THINGS WE DON'T TALK ABOUT

(after Caitlin Conlon)

The nights of pretending Yes / the Empath who's a
Narcissist / that 3 am with the knife and the cops /
the blood on the walls / how he thinks the scars are
my fault / how that might be true / his alphabetized
incest porn / her shrouded noose / salt-covered
wooden spoons / lying about rape / saying nothing
when it happens / replacing kisses with cigarettes /
ghosting as a request for changed behaviour / sex
as validation for the fragile ego / guilt about not
reporting when he strikes again / community as self-
sabotage / food as intimacy / emulating misogyny
to join the boys' club / casual sex stories that pry
open your thighs / "safe" spaces that retraumatize /
lies that win slams / envying the person you appear
to be on Instagram / waiting for fame to call /
attention as the most potent drug of them all.

WHEN HE IS NOT SORRY

When he is not sorry,
and that is all you want to hear.

When he is not sorry,
and that is what your body
keeps screaming for.

When he will not apologize
because he does not understand
the seed he planted in you
or the miscarriage he triggered.

When they tell you to forgive him,
and you try, but you can't because
forgiving him is all you've ever done.

When he is not sorry,
what else can you do but forgive yourself
for trying to get blood from a stone wall
disguising as an open gateway?

When he is not sorry,
but you need someone to hear
the silent screams of your womb
that trusts again and again,
that opens again and again,
that ignores neglect
to erect a straw sanctuary.

When he is not sorry,
I will feel it with you:
the depth of your longing,
the height of your fantasies,
the fortitude of your fervent faith.
I will feel what he cannot.

I will bear your ectopic love
inside both my ovaries,
give birth to mangled hopes.

I will not sell you on detached spirituality.
I will not preach objectivity,
smear sentiments in the mud.

It happened; it is real, no matter
who has ignored it or for how long.
Your ache can sit at my table.
We will feed it memories.
We will fatten your trauma
until it can eat no more
and lies down to hibernate.

Who else would know
to heal a wound this way
except one of us cicatrix sisters:
bellies blemished by barrage,
sinuses scorched by beseechment?

When he is not sorry,
do not keep searching
for one more word
to help him understand.

You've had enough.

It's enough.

Come home.

PORN IS NOT SEX EDUCATION

I gripe about
being unsatisfied
but being objectified
is my comfort zone.

I am in control
when I consent
to being his fantasy.

I am terrified
of the vulnerability
required to receive
(or even ask for)
what I want.

—*Why do I say "Fuck me" when I mean "Slow down"?*

BAD SEX

When he says
he thought you wanted it.
When he says
he thought it was consensual,
and you start
to feel dumb, do not go back.

You've started talking. Finish it.

Tell him
sex isn't a Yes or No question.
Tell him
he is all bass and no melody.
Tell him
you are tired of dancing to half a song.

You want more. Admit it.

When he asks
if you want it, confused,
tell him
sex is not a Yes or No question.
Tell him
your pleasure matters.

Your fantasies are not frivolous.

When he says
the same is true for him too,
and you start
to feel dumb, do not go back.

Believe you deserve more.

When you get lonely,
return to your fingertips, serenade yourself.

When you consider eating your words,
imagine the next woman he will disappoint.

        Teach the truth, sister. Don't spread the lies.

And when you envision
the terrible violations we have suffered,
and you wonder
whether these nights of bad sex are a real problem,

               remember this:

every avalanche
contains trillions of snowflakes and
every snowflake
contains trillions of water molecules.

              Change is change.

              Respect is respect.

              It all matters.

TURN AROUND. THE DOOR IS UNLOCKED.

The walls of this prison
are padded with excuses
left behind by my mother
and her mother
and all the women who,
for centuries, have scratched
the walls, counting the days
with quiet rage.

LOVE AND GASLIGHT

Kush, kombucha, and ketamine,
probiotics, prayers, and unchecked privilege,
burn sage, breathe deep, and blame the victims.

Downward dog and don't jump to conclusions,
meditate and must have misunderstood,
microdose and let the microaggressions slide.

Cocaine, quinoa, and cultural appropriation,
pineal gland, psytrance, and implicit bias,
trauma bond, tone police, and trust yourself.

Sprouted grains and spiritual bypassing,
unshaved armpits and unreported assaults,
ostracize whistleblowers and open your third eye.

NOTE TO SELF #10

Beautiful isn't something
you become.
Beautiful is something
you realize
you are.

RAZOR CULT

Sister,
if he
wants to touch
that exquisite and rare diamond
between your legs,
if he
wants to slip into
that honey they swarm around,
always hungry, always go,
then he will take it
however you give it to him.
And if you want to give it to him hairy,
that's how he's going to fucking take it.

—Stop trying so hard. Find your own beautiful.

NOBODY'S LITTLE WIFE

I have been the secret
almost as often as I've been the trophy.
Neither fits me, so why
do I go along with every boy's story
of who I should be?

The side chick, the girlfriend,
the fuck friend, the whore—
who am I trying so hard for?

The eyes I face on judgment day
will be my own.

I am the one
who must unleash my creative potential.
Their opinions are inconsequential.
Their voices can't take a residential
role in my life.

I will not arrive
to my sunsets
half-alive.

I will dive
deep and thrive.

I am
nobody's
little wife.

THESE ARE THE DAYS

These are the days of
sitting like a bird on a power line,
claws around 10,000 volts,
ungrounded but stable,
safe in the sky.

These are the days of
repeating, "Did I say
you could touch me?"
whenever necessary,
like teaching a child
to say please and thank you.

These are the days of
saying please and thank you.

These are the days of
"I have something
I've wanted to talk to you about
for a while now."

The days of
making choices
without awaiting permission
from people I've attracted into my life
to disapprove of my brightest light.

The days of
excavating trauma's magnets
out of my muscles, so I can stop
cutting myself on the barbed wire
that gets stuck to my rib cage
every time I trespass over my boundaries.

These are the days of
not trespassing over my boundaries.

The days of
"Here's where I'm comfortable
with you touching me."
And if you don't know how,
these are the days of not teaching.

The days of
getting up and leaving.

The days of
saying, "No."

The days of
figuring out what I want to say "Yes" to.

The days of
"I just want to dance with myself right now...
...but you can watch...
...from over there."

These are the days of
lying in the sunlight,
reading in the lamplight,
singing in the moonlight.

These are the days of
long naps and short words.

The days of
not explaining why, why, why
to those looking for a reaction,
not an answer.

The days of
holding myself, pleasing myself,
not waiting for someone else
to draw masterpieces on my skin.

The days of
mending shattered bones
and stitching gaping wounds.

The days of
"This is what I'm looking for
in a partner, and if I don't find it,
I'm perfectly happy alone."

And meaning it.

Really meaning it.

2

SMOKE

NOTE TO SELF #11

Stop gorging
on rejection.

Stop taking
the doubt they break you with
and using it to break yourself.

Let people's reactions
represent them,
not you.

Shine.

SCREAMING SECRETS

Silence never knew how to keep mum
or daddy's secrets for that matter

over mind hidden in a box in the attic,
something up there always fell over

or died, and there it was, every time
piece sprung forward, ready to clean

up was always the only way to rise
and shine, the only way to avoid

holes marked filled but only covered
up and down and still and deep.

WHERE ARE YOU FROM?

A few years ago,
my ex-country waltzed into world news
wearing nothing but war.

"A cheap way to go viral,"
some said.
"What a whore."

They ask,
"Which parts have you grazed?"
Like teenage boys
hungry for parked car confessions.

My answer
sounds like a question.

They gape.
"Her Kiev, did you say?
My cousin said his friend fondled her Kiev once."

Their questions
sound like answers.

They ask,
"Have you seen her again since you left?"
Like numb-brained housewives
hungry for formulaic romance.

My answer
sounds like a mistake.

PRETTY AND THIN

The first time I threw up to feel skinny, I was five
          years old. My grandmother still thinks this is
a funny story: a little girl lies about being sick to get

babushka's syrup of ipecac, bows to porcelain,
          runs to the mirror, asks, "Don't I look pretty?
Don't I look thin?" Cue laughter. Everyone's amused.

Except me. If that's how it started, it's no wonder
          how it ended. Has it ended? I say an eating
disorder is something I *had*, like it's an old sweater

I misplaced during a move, but I don't talk about
          days ruined by seeing my reflection
in a store window or orgasms that never happened

because I was too busy trying to fold my stretch
          marks into the sheets, tuck my razor burn
under the pillow—if you love me, turn off the lights

so I can't worry about the differences I assume you
          notice between me and the Perfect Tens.
I'm thirsty, but I won't admit to feeling disgusted by

those who bring me water. It's a comfort thing:
          my indifference addiction. I never learned to
receive, and I often take social problems personally.

How can I judge my mother for saying I was too fat,
          too big, don't eat that, don't eat this, if I still
do it to myself? How can I keep these secrets when

there are children out there who puke up breakfast
          to feel pretty and thin? We huff and puff on
saran-wrapped beauty, plastic and all; and then we

wonder why our courage gets wrinkly long before
our skin does. We live and die feeling ugly,
and we don't talk about it. But shouldn't we? Isn't it

time? Don't these kids deserve to know our sickness
by name, so they can never call it health?

IF YOU (DON'T) FIND ME AGAIN

Remember to leave a promise in each vertebra
so when they ask me when the pain started,
I remember you when I don't tell them
I don't know. I've never known.

Write your questions in blood—yes, that kind—
stuff them into an envelope, seal it.
Write the words you never told me on the front.
Erase them poorly. Erase them just enough.

Tell the courier that truth has no postal code,
but there is a King Street in every city.
Tell me to pick it up. Say it's an emergency.
Make me wait. Make me pay the customs fees.

Remember to leave your scent all over my passport
so when they ask about the purpose of my visit,
I remember you when I don't tell them
I don't know. I've never known.

Ask where it hurts
so you can forget,
ask for forgiveness
so it never heals.

NOMAD PALETTE

The word *stranger*
is as salty as
the word *immigrant*.

The meanings I blend
are as overpowering as
the ones I inherited.

The word *displacement*
is as bitter as
the word *home*.

EXCHANGE RATES

If I had a ruble for every time
     I disappointed my family,
I could buy one shot of cheap vodka
     per every three hundred failures.
But I quit drinking shots.

If I had a gryvnia for every time
     I disappointed my family,
I could buy one pack of cheap tobacco
     per every three hundred aches.
But I quit smoking cigarettes.

If I had a dollar for every time
     I disappointed my family,
I still wouldn't have enough money
     to buy a ticket back home.
But I quit making excuses.

If I had a penny for every time
     I disappointed myself,
I could pay to fly my whole family
     to Donetsk and back.
But I quit bartering love.

THEY JUST WANT TO KNOW

Why don't you visit more often?

Have you gained weight?

When are you going to stop wasting time,
get a house, have some babies?

You did so well in school, Nika.
You could have been a doctor. Now,
you're living on the edge of poverty.
Pfft, poetry? You speak three languages.
Why don't you translate instead?

What are you wearing? It's embarrassing.
We could run into people I work with.

Why don't you write thrillers?
That's where the real money is.

Art? You think you're going to be an artist?
And what if you can't? You think everyone
who puts their mind to something does it?
You think everyone who believes in
themselves gets what they want?

Paying, are you? What, did you win the lottery?

Really though, have you gained weight.
Can't find a gym nearby?

What is that thing on your face?

Why don't you visit more often?

WHY (NOT) ME

We couldn't all be doctors and peasants.
      Someone had to be a poet.
We couldn't all marry the same paper money.
      Someone had to throw coins in the well.
We couldn't all stop washing dishes by hand.
      Someone had to gas leak the dream home.
We couldn't all relish the taste of assimilation.
      Someone had to spit.

NOTE TO SELF #12

Healing rarely looks good.

Let them turn up their noses
at your closed buds
and dirty petals.

Share soil with those
who do not demand more grace,
who let you bloom.

RESERVED FOR MY SOULMATE

idealism
Working memory can hold 3 to 7 items at once.
That's 3 to 7 VIP seats in my attention span.
One is permanently reserved for you.
It's always unoccupied.

sadism
We assume cats love laser pointers.
What if they hate chasing an unattainable dot?
What if it's a reflex like a knee jerk?
We call it play.

stigmatism
Your flaws ambush the VIP section.
They get kicked out, as usual.
I didn't hire this security guard.
There is safety in loving an empty chair.

schism
Don't dangle tenderness in front of my face
if you're not going to feed it to me.
Don't wave the scent of home around.
It's cruel, and I might bite.

cataclysm
I lock the guard out of the building.
Your flaws are staying for the show tonight.
You're not here, as usual.
I am sitting in your seat.

WATCHING OLD RUSSIAN MOVIES
WITH MY MOTHER

She says, "I don't like this scene." I ask why.
She groans a little, says, "It's just... you'll see."

All I can say is "That didn't look consensual."
She says, "That's how it was back home."

After the next one, I groan, repeat myself.
"That didn't look consensual either. "

She says, "I'm telling you,
that's how it always was back home.
This is where we come from.
This is what we're dealing with."

We both exhale until we are empty;
we exhale a little more.

She rasps, "That's the whole problem."

SOUTHBOUND

Today, my GPS was pointing in the wrong direction, so I looked up which way West was, in case my map was magnetized toward you. It wasn't. I keep giving magic the upper hand on logic while your disinterest draws me like a moth to a buzzing UV light. I'm not the only bug here; it's not your job to stop glowing. When day breaks, I'm trekking out East. Unnoticed coincidences are just events. Unfulfilled fantasies are just thoughts. They say an illusion is something you experience while a delusion is something you think, but I didn't invent the way you looked at me. I misinterpreted it. I've always been good at making things up. If you told me right now that you love me, I'd believe it. I'd know it wasn't true, but I'd believe it all the same. The illusion is heartbreak; the delusion is deserving it. No compass has answers to questions I am afraid to ask. Like, was any of it real? Like, do you ever think about me? If you go far enough East, you end up where West was. But if you go far enough North, you might just forget. But do you want to? But what, in the end, draws us anywhere? And what, in the end, is irrefutably real?

RECOVERY

I ruminate on the guillotine fondly,
imagine its chill on my neck.

My restraining-order conscience:
a paper shield in an armed world.

I muse my fate in Technicolor,
saturate the odds and ends.

My trauma-addict imagination:
hoarding my verve for a stranger.

I save up my lightning for his night,
hold back my thunder for her day.

My wolf-who-cried-girl silence:
I wear it like a bulletproof vest.

I drink solitude to stay sober,
pierce loneliness into my tongue.

My hard-earned, runaway freedom:
how I brood over my beloved prison cell.

I listen to the past post-mortem.
It sounds so eager for today.

MY ONLY UKRAINIAN FRIEND

When she visited her birth city,
she forgave her father
because she discovered
that all the men in our country
are the same flavour of awful.

NO ONE KNEW US LIKE WE DID

The falling leaves remind me of the months before Christmas at your parents' house, curled around each other in a twin bed, waking up every few hours to turn around. I never sat your family down to break up with them. We knew it was our last holiday together. You convinced me not to tell them. Not your first denial. Not our first secrecy. We were always so good at appearing to be happy. The wind howls. Winter is coming. It's May. I didn't bring enough sweaters for winter in May. I didn't marinate enough youth for new hope. I don't miss that tiny twin bed that didn't fit us. I miss a future where we laugh about it together. This winter will have no Christmas. It will end in Labour Day. I will be a little older. Where you are, the leaves will begin falling. You will sleep on the twin bed alone. Your mother will ask about me. My grandmother will ask about you. You'll make a joke about the bed. No one will laugh like me. You will cry. I will too, but you will never know. Nothing will patch the seven-year hole in our hearts. I want to tell you about the book I'm reading. You want to tell me about your latest trip. But the leaves will fall. We will stay silent, cry alone. And one day, there will be nothing left not to say.

THIGH TRAP

Sometimes, I'm having a good day until I see my
thighs in a storefront window, and it begins—
pathogenic, debilitating shame.

I stop looking women in the eyes. My ego seesaws
between "I'm glad my thighs aren't that bad"
and "I'd die to have thighs like hers."

I want to go home, put on pants, stock up weapons:
full-length mirrors, scales, and bright lights,
coffee, calories, and cigarettes.

Instead, I reminisce about my thighs carrying me:
forest paths, dance floors, and mountains,
stages, beaches, and airport gates.

Even with all the insults I have shouted at my thighs,
they still *carry me*. They *still* carry me.
(More than anyone else has.)

I find another shop window. Instead of looking
at my thighs, I fall into my big, blue eyes
and say, "I'm *sorry*." And I am.

SURVIVAL

It was called *obshedzitiye*. Google says that word means "dormitory." Replace students with families, put one tiny kitchen in each room, move the only shower in the building into the basement, add a lot of bugs, and there you go: *obshedzitiye*.

Each floor also had one big kitchen. My friend and I snuck in there every chance we got. We once found a folded-up chessboard; an entire civilization of cockroaches poured out. What was her name?

She and I found what we decided were apple seeds on the kitchen floor. I still eat apple cores, so eating the seeds was probably my idea. That night, it took a lot of syrup of ipecac and hours of heaving before the last bit of cockroach poison was safely out of our stomachs. They were angry, but my parents couldn't even hit me. They laughed and laughed. So I did too.

When a friend took my cookie, my dad taught me how to fight. My fist whizzed through the air. Do it again. Harder. Do it again. Never, ever trust anyone. Again. Was it the same friend? Did I see her again?

My mom caught two huge rats and put them in a cage with a big piece of cheese before we went to visit my grandparents. When we came back, we found one dead rat and one tail. Even after they explained what happened, I didn't cry. They laughed and laughed. So I did too.

TRAILBLAZING AND TORTURE

Nobody talks about this part.

They tell you about the stitches:
how they come undone,
how they bleed through all your clothes.

They don't tell you about the wind:
how it gestates amnesia and palpates limbo,
how it howls for the one who broke you.

They tell you about the ghost:
how it digs itself out of the grave,
how it slashes your scars with razor thumbs.

They don't tell you about twilight:
how it crawls into the cracks between violence,
how it yearns for the war it calls soil.

They tell you about time:
how it hides under the bed for centuries,
how it comes out when it's ready.

They don't tell you about space:
how it loses its voice screaming into the vacuum,
how it bursts into universes to avoid singularity.

Nobody talks about this part,
homesick for prison food.

Nobody talks about
wasted hope.

NOTE TO SELF #13

Change is not something you do.
Change is something you allow.

SILENT DEMOGRAPHICS

No one notices the Matrushka doll
    until she lisps through a sliced tongue
hand-painted doubt sitting neatly on the windowsill
    until she listens with a hammered eardrum
until the cat knocks her over
    until you twist her open again and again
and all her insides fall out

No one sees the prayer beads
    until you ask how deep the Volga river runs
made of knuckles and sanded fangs
    until you ask how tall the Ural mountains are
until she asks the sky questions
    until you hear her croon fables
in a language no one speaks

No one fears the old woman
    until her broom sweeps their pupils
with crooked manners and hairy intuition
    until her pestle grinds their cartilage
until her hut stretches its chicken legs
    until their radio mythology trembles
and runs off into the sunset

No one pities the pickled red herring
    until she smears mustard on her painting
with a mayonnaise accent and beet-stained teeth
    until she drinks out of the bathtub
until her words cook themselves
    until she snorts flour for dessert
just in time for tea

GIRLS

1. We get caught shoplifting. The cops ask me if I have scars, tattoos, or previous crimes. They ask her where she lives. It was her idea, but who'd believe it? We get into a fight at recess. She screams, "Why don't you go eat something?" I scream, "Why don't you go cut yourself some more?" Or maybe we both stay silent, on the verge of tears, while the whole school gathers around us in the hallway, and boys scream about cutting and eating. Either way, we stop being friends.

2. She teaches me to straighten my hair with a towel and a clothing iron. She brings me to where the boys hang out. I answer questions when asked, but never how they want me to. They share their liquor. We share our lies. When the cops come, the boys run off. We get a ticket. We skip school to go to court. The judge groans, waives the fine. "They left you there," he reminds us, "all of them," shakes his head. I get grounded for running away from home. She stops talking to me.

3. We buy cigarettes together. She lends me her makeup. She has the best stuff. When I say I like someone, she flirts with him. Whenever we have an audience, we make out. She won't kiss me if no one is watching. I meet my first boyfriend, and she sits on his lap in the cafeteria. Years later, I ask someone what happened to her. He says she ended up fat, pregnant, and living on the reserve. He laughs. I don't.

4. She stands up on the first day of grade 9 English talking about Homeward Bound. "Bunnies," she says, "the lives of bunnies." Everybody thinks she's an idiot. I hang out with her after school. She lives in a house with her boyfriend. They have cigarettes and everything. I sit on a worn red leather chair listening to them fuck. A week later, her boyfriend is away, but his twin brother is visiting. He hits on me for hours. I don't tell her, but I swear the "twins" are the same person. One day, she stops coming to school. No one asks why.

"AND... WHERE IS YOUR DAUGHTER?"

He tells me I'm a Good Girl, says I have strong legs, winks at me every time I look at his side of the table. It's so obvious, and he's so old, I start laughing. He changes his offer. He says, "My son is strong like you." I laugh harder. No one else gets the joke. He calls me young. They mutter how many cars he owns. He shows off his Bentley in the driveway, says it's the same age as I am. He calls me beautiful. The host shrugs and says, "You met his specs." When I catch my breath, I reply, "I like being alone, thanks." He chuckles, "You say this now, but you're going to get old soon!" I know I should be grimacing, but I'm laughing. Maybe his son would get it. Wouldn't they all pretend not to understand then? While I'm in the bathroom, he tells my mother I'm "strong but crazy" and that she's the only sane woman around. Does she laugh? At the end of the night, he asks me to tie his shoes because he just had a kidney operation. And you know something? I get down on my knees and tie that man's shoelaces. That's what happened. I don't think this makes me any less of a feminist. ...Do you?

NOTE TO MY NINE-YEAR-OLD SELF

They call you weird.
Nikushka, it's a compliment.
They call you crazy.
Nikulya, all the best artists are.

KOLOBOK / MY THOUGHTS ON MARRIAGE

Dedushka Misha used to come home,
vodka and cigarettes on his tongue,
ask me to scratch his back. In return,
he'd tell me folktales about Ivan,
the foolish boy who lived on top of
the fireplace, about Baba Yaga
with her crooked nose and forest hut,
and, my favourites, fables about a little
ball of dough named Kolobok who
rolled out the window, seeking freedom.

Kolobok's adventures consisted of
escaping various animals who tried
to eat him: the rabbit, the fox, the bear,
the wolf. Kolobok had a jingle he'd sing
as he made yet another cunning escape.

Singing ball of dough aside, I wonder
which is the bigger fiction: that
Kolobok is male or that escaping
predators can be an enjoyable,
sing-song adventure. Either way,
in my grandpa's stories, Kolobok
would come back at the end,
ready to be made into bread.

I'm telling you now:
no matter how many
animals I have to escape,
I'm not going into that oven.

THE UNWRITTEN REVOLUTION IN FIVE ACTS

Characters

a mother full of unpainted landscapes
with a graveyard full of boundaries
and an echo that's never kind

a father full of uncarved furniture
with a wreckage full of chemistry
and a heart that never forgives

a child full of unspoken words
with a wastebasket full of almost
and eye contact that's never there

Plot

Act I: exposition
how quiet a child can be during an eruption

Act II: rising action
how quiet a child can be while screaming for help

Act III: climax
how loud a child can be inside a helicopter

Act IV: falling action
how loud a mother can be while screaming over
helicopter blades

Act V: dénouement
how quiet a mother can be while waiting for her
own helicopter to come

THIRD SUNDAY OF JUNE

You seemed pleased to see me,
said you liked my hair,
and for a second, I regretted
putting my hand in it all—

the mirrors I held
to your sleights of soul,
the evidence I kept
of your covered-up crimes,
the idioms I invented
to decode your holographic heart,
the flights I arranged
to get her off your shipwreck—

but then you had a few drinks,
made your jokes,
told your lies,
showed us your new toys
(all the ways you bribe loneliness when it haunts),
wrapped her around your finger
(just to show you still could),
told me I really must grow my hair back

and if it wasn't so sad,
it would be funny

and if I didn't love you,
I would hate you

and if I could convince my cells to stop hungering
for your processed, poisonous, pinky-ringed rapport,
I would never speak to you again.

TEENAGE FLASHBACK

The cop drops me off around the corner
so the neighbours won't talk,
but it was never the neighbours
I was worried about.

The door goes click, clack.
I can't bring myself to open it.
I want to ask the officer to
drop me off around the corner
of Time and Coincidence
where a plot twist reveals
that I was adopted.

It's possible. Maybe I was sent away
by a family in Canada to Ukraine.
They did it for a reason I can't fathom
but will find effortless to forgive later.
Any day now, they will come for me.

I promise to be a better daughter
for parents who look me in the eyes.

IQ TESTING FOR THE GIFTED PROGRAM

What's the Order?

five photos (get your story straight)
sunrise to sunset (don't be lazy)
unplowed to plowed field (finish the job)

What's Missing?

a pencil without lead (freedom of speech)
an airplane with one wing (empathy)
a kite without a string (gratitude)

What's the Order?

ten numbers (measure moments in amounts)
21, 3, 0, 1, 13, 2, 8, 34, 1, 5 (seek patterns in chaos)
bonus to label it (read textbooks after school)

What's Missing?

five letters or less (most of our last names)
eight letters or more (the rest of our last names)
application to testing (only by request)

PLAYING HOUSE

Let's play a game. Father always goes first. Father picks up all the cards. Father chooses trump. Father chooses how many cards to give to Mother and Child. Giving cards is optional. Mother and Child should be satisfied to simply watch Father play with himself and win. Father never loses.

When Father is gone, Mother must take Father's role, taking all the cards and choosing which to give to Child. Mother should take care to perform Father's role seamlessly.

When Child leaves, she should find someone to play Father while she plays Mother. She must get sick of this and play Father instead. She must hate herself afterward.

Child should shun the cards. She could learn another game, but she won't. She is tired of sitting at the table. She packs her bags, parts her lips, whistles in Bb, and keeps her hands ever empty. Father calls it betrayal.

Back home, they are still playing the game. The cards have frayed beyond recognition. Mother sometimes wants to know who will inherit all the rules. Mother sometimes thinks of singing. Mother sometimes thinks of running away.

NOTE TO SELF #14

Those who cling to
their cocoons will
criticize how
you use your wings.
Let them.
Keep flying.

PASS THE SALT AND GO FUCK YOURSELF.

You've always been too sensitive / he's a nice guy / you must have misunderstood / you must have done something / he would never / you must remember it wrong / you're overreacting / why didn't you leave sooner if it was so bad / I'm glad you've learned your lesson / I know exactly how you feel / that's just like the time I spilled my milk three years ago / he's got a heart of gold / let's talk about something less controversial / everyone gets what they deserve / you shouldn't feel that way / what did you do to provoke it / you receive what you attract / we all know he meant well / he's such a nice guy / you've always been much too sensitive.

PASS THE PEPPER AND SHUT THE FUCK UP.

I know a guy who came to this country with $10 and now he's a millionaire / I don't care if you're green or purple / nothing ever changes / there's no justice in this world / everyone who works hard gets rewarded / everyone gets what they deserve / he was on drugs though / I have bigger problems / I don't know why you have to bring politics into everything / you know he doesn't mean anything by it / I don't know why you can't just be nice / he had to say that word to tell the story / how else do you tell the story / where do you get your numbers from / let me show you this Polish guy at the airport / now that's sad / now that's a real tragedy.

FISH / WHY DO YOU CARE

The first time I saw a dead fish, I was six.
Maybe I'd seen one before, but that day
at the market in Donetsk, I *saw* a dead fish
on the floor and put it in my pocket. Later,
I put it in a bowl of water, wrapped bandages
around its feeble scales, puffed over its gills.
My grandmother watched me. I remember
the moment when I learned that some
things can't be fixed. Years later, I
wondered why she let me try so hard.

The last time I went fishing, I was nine, at
a friend's cottage in Ontario. I suggested
putting them into a pot with lake water.
I left to use the toilet. When I returned,
all the fish were dead. When I asked
why she didn't release them, she said,
"I wanted to see what you'd say." I
dumped the pot into the lake, floating
faux pas. I remember the moment
I learned that a suggestion can become
an execution order. Years later, I wondered
how she could have watched them die.

I never considered eating any of those
fish. Are you listening? I'm telling you
I *never* even *considered* eating *any*
of those fish.

Does that answer your question?

A GIRL AT AN AFTER-PARTY ASKS

"What do you think about some Ukrainians
not wanting to be part of Russia?"

I try to tell her what I remember.

She interrupts.
"But what do you think about some Ukrainians
not wanting to be part of Russia?"

I try to tell her what I think home is.

She interrupts.
"But really, I've been researching it, and
I want to know: what is your opinion
about some of these Ukrainians
not wanting to be part of Russia?"

I tell her I respect when people
feel they belong somewhere.

She is silent for a moment.

"So you don't have an opinion then?"

1

BURN

NOTE TO SELF #15

Stop combing the woods after midnight,
hoping your old body will turn up.
It won't. It's gone.

It's gone forever and no amount
of sparkly self-help unicorn bullshit
will ever bring it back.

But know this: starting today,
your soul can get pregnant again,
birth a new innocence.

It might be bittersweet: the first time
you see its face, caress its little fists.
You might recollect what is gone.

But one day, you will be too busy
loving your hand-stitched heart
to miss your unbroken one.

THAT FRESH FACT FLAVOUR

Sometimes it's sweet,
fingers clasped around my shoulders,
sweaty, swaddled, and a little
surprised at the strength of my hands.

Sometimes, it's salty.
It retains water, holds back tears,
doesn't let go until the dam
is ready for flash floods.

Sometimes, it's spicy,
discomfort churns, burns, turns to fire
and runs deep, deep down
to that phoenix spot, the one
that makes sparks from ashes.

Sometimes, it's sour.
It burns. I swear I won't do it again,
but as soon as the tang wanes,
I thirst for more.

Sometimes, it's bitter.
It is not a fairy tale.
It's ugly and incomplete.
It's hollow but, without it,
I can't trust the day.

Sometimes, it tastes
like nothing at all.
That is the only part
I truly cannot stand.

SOLVING FOR SEX

The first mistake is nostalgia for the
burning belly, concussion days. I was

a singing, dancing chemical reaction.
But I let people brush by me, didn't I?

And couldn't I get a pap smear without
shaking behind the clinic afterward?

The second mistake is trying to figure
out when it started, which leads to

remembering all the ways it never stopped.
The third mistake is trying to imagine

what recovery looks like. I'm always wrong.
The fourth mistake is selective obsession.

I am hung up on my last poemless kiss
and not my last kissless poem. I wanted

my last kiss to be love. I wanted my last
love poem to be a magic spell. Nothing

I want is what it seems. The last mistake
is pretending I don't want anything.

The last mistake is no more mistakes.

IF MY SKIN COULD SPEAK

If my skin could speak,
it would probably start by
giving me the silent treatment.

If my skin could speak,
it would tell you about all those who
haven't heard the *No* my body screams
but my lips never utter.

Don't touch me
is my skin's native dialect,
but no one speaks that language,
(especially not my tongue)
so I'll wait until you're done.

You'll be gone in the morning when
I blame my hearticidal hangover ideations
on drinking too many of your expectations
and not chasing with any of mine.

If my vagina could speak,
she would tell you about when
the tunnels of my temple
heard a Hymn, felt a Him:
a looping song, a loophole boy,
an anthem to something lost,
a one-hit-wonder no one ever
plays on the jukebox.
...except me.

If my vagina could speak,
she would tell you stories
about all those who left a mess,
overstayed, how I invited them all.

She'd tell you how I remind her
that looping a word over and over
makes it lose its meaning,
so I looped him in my life hoping that if I said
I like it, I like it, I like it, I like it enough times,
it would stop sounding like a lie.

If my thighs could speak,
they'd mumble about my shame marks
and how I shave off my fallopian accent
before I go swimming with the sharks,
but I forget they can smell me
(even when I dress in hoodies,
they still call me sweetie),
and how the skin underneath
is Braille he touches but doesn't read.

If my thighs could speak,
they'd plead for fingers with literacy.

If my fingers could speak,
they'd tell you how I burned my biography,
swept the ashes under the carpet,
painted my walls pretty, sealed leaks in my honesty
but nothing can fix a smile that's broken
because I'm choking on words stuck in my windpipe.

If my lungs could speak,
they'd tell you I inhale everything but clean air,
how singing teachers tell me to breathe lower,
but I am afraid to send breath to the parts of me
I silenced in the middle of their testimonies,
terrified of belting out the lyrics to my history.

If my ears could speak,
they'd ask for headphones to dull out the drone
of cat-calls-to-action-reaction-conquering
and poems with promises to please me
and all the other relationship resumes
by applicants not qualified to operate
my innocence back together again.

If my skin could speak,
it would write poems about numbness.
It would tell you about hushed ice ages
that trap every living seed under the snow
and nothing blooms until he walks out the door.

If my skin could speak,
It would ask me why self-respect
has become a synonym for sleeping alone.
It would hope that someone could help me translate
these manuscripts of fear and pain
into poetry about integrity reclaimed.

If my skin could speak,
and you listened,
it would say,
"The End."

It would say,
"Now that I'm done talking,
I'm ready to trust again."

I FORGIVE YOU

Where does love sleep when fear bursts in,
gaze hungry, hands up, words blazing?
Where does love go after fear burns down
every last straw, and there's nowhere

to hide from the cold? I used to believe
that real love never needed a blanket,
that it burned bright like the Sun.
But love is both. It is both especially

for creatures like us, so much like every
galactic body, every living thing,
yet we are endowed with this disturbing
and heavy gift of questioning everything.

We wander lost, searching for home,
and when we discover it in each other,
we feel more lost than ever.
Your starry sky, my burning bonfire.

No fire struggles to keep burning.
No sky struggles to stay vast.
But we are both. We are both,
especially creatures like us

who ooze with art, crave perfection,
swoon for elegance, lick around the real,
never quite able to leave it alone.
What a catastrophe. What a masterpiece.

RAVAGE THE RAINBOW

I want to taste you.

I want to drink the rivers that run through my valleys
and back into your ocean.

Take me to where it smells like water,
where the earth is soft and moist,
and I don't know if I'm sweating or crying,
but let's soak your sheets and forget to stay quiet
for neighbours who have never heard real rain.

Tell me how we got here.

Tell me again about that time I tilted my chin back,
stuck out my tongue, and swallowed raindrops.

Take my hand, you perfect storm.

Quiver with me through this hurricane.

Let's evaporate our fantasies until our clouds swell
with the promise of thunder.

Pour with me.

Spill every last drop.

Collapse into the puddles.

Take me into your sky
and tell me
this,
this,
this
is what a rainbow looks like.

NOTE TO SELF #16

The road is long in every direction.
Whether you follow someone else's footsteps
or blaze your own trail, the road is still long.

Walk the one that is howling for you.

Go now. It is never too late.
Even if you must turn around
and go back the way you came,
you cannot go backwards.

The path will not look the same walking North
as it did walking South.

You will not be the same person facing the sunset
as you were turning your back to it.

Go now.

Your destiny yearns for you
as much as you yearn for it.

Find your magic.

Live.

Rise.

THE DAYS OF HER RISE

When love songs remind you
of your reflection,
when you miss no one
and the sky kisses your bones,
then, you know
the healing has rooted.
Then, you know
you have found
your way home.

—*As Long As You LA-La-La-LA-La-Love Me*

PROGRESS

I sprout tiny flowers.

I've been digging compost,
exhuming bones,
planting dirty seeds
I kept refrigerated
for someday, someday.

Now, they are blooming.
I'm nervous they'll die.
Everything I love dies.
I don't say this aloud.

I smile, close my eyes,
whisper heartsick hopes
to the wild, West wind.

All I have lost is faith
in an old love story.
But it was due for a rewrite.

I am tired of tragedy.
I can't stand Shakespeare.
I don't want the kind of love
where we both die at the end.

These flowers are too precious
to end up pressed between the pages
of someone else's diary.
They're small, but they're mine.

I still reek of dirt.

I like it.

CLOSURE

I have nightmares. You're feeble-kneed and furious. You're spitting disgust all over my cheeks. You're lisping *pathetic* over blasting music, throwing metal over-the-door hooks at my face, hissing *worthless* in an underground bowling alley bar. You're collapsed on the cement pathway beside the recycling bins. You're screaming at me on the corner of Yonge and College, and I'm telling you to get in the cab, and there are people everywhere, and I don't make eye contact with them when you call me a slut. I tell you to get in the cab. I wake up and you're sick all over the pillows. I wake up and you're looking at me with apologetic eyes. I wake up and, once again, you're promising never again. I wake up, ready to leave, and you're threatening to stab me. I wake up alone in a two-person tent to the sound of splashing waves and chirping Blue Jays. I grasp my chest to feel my heartbeat, and it's over. It wasn't a dream. It was a synopsis. The nightmare is over. I'm haunted by reruns, but they're victories. My flashbacks are medals in a battle no one knows I won.

IS THAT...? COULDN'T BE.

surrender
I hurt myself so much today, it finally
bleeds. I fall to my knees. Something
catches me and holds me—I mean
really holds me. It speaks. *He* speaks.

logic
I ran into the arms of a disembodied
"Him" because I had no good men
to run to. It's sad, isn't it? We invent
imaginary humans to make up for
the ones we lack in the real world.

truth
I've had a Him-sized hole my entire life.
I assumed that hole lived between my legs,
but every Him I cried for in the middle of
the night never came or, worse, came
and then rolled over.

guilt
My grandfather tells me religious people
back in the USSR were considered
mentally ill. I tell him I'm neither religious
nor afraid of being labelled mentally ill,
but it's weird talking to someone I don't see.

surrender
Talking to you helps. I'm still not sure if
you're just a figment of my imagination,
but hey, if it works, it works. What can
I say? Thank you.

...NOW

It sneaks up slowly: the brush of But
against my shoulder, the murmur of Why

faint in my ear, the clocking of 9 hours
but I'm still tired from nightmare dreams

with eyes-taped-shut reruns of secrets
that keep secreting. I tell my reflection

it's a sign of progress. I tore open stitches
over infected wounds. "You knew it would

hurt," I say. She replies, "I didn't realize it
would all come at once." I want to remind her

how much worse it could be. I don't. She
sees my peace flag, blinks, doesn't ask How.

We're both in for one of those eggshells
in the pan, yolk all over the stove kind of days.

I look in the mirror and say, "I've got you."
She narrows her eyes as I conjure up

nights when I broke into my bone marrow,
stole every treasure, sold it for a Wow or two,

climbed back into bed, woke up shocked
that everything valuable was suddenly

gone. "You blamed me," she seethes.
I don't pretend I didn't. I say, "I've got you

...now. I promise. I'm here ...now."

HEALING LOOKS DIFFERENT EVERY DAY

Last week,
I wrote letters to the people who made it worse.

Eight days ago,
one called and apologized.

Seven days ago,
I stopped believing.

Six days ago,
I let someone hold me for the first time in months.

Five days ago,
I shaved my head and felt beautiful again.

Four days ago,
at the airport, I looked men in the eyes with no fear.

Three days ago,
I kneeled in grass, ate a red pepper, believed again.

Two days ago,
I wrote forgiveness letters, inhaled, couldn't sleep.

Yesterday,
awaiting test results, I imagined dying, felt relieved.

Last night,
I exhaled, gave up on believing.

Today,
I woke up stretching my heart to fit all this new bliss.

A few hours ago,
I didn't just believe—I knew.

Tomorrow,
I might write a forgiveness letter to myself.

FORGIVE THOSE MEN, BABY. FOR YOU.

I forgive you, father,
for not seeing who I am
beneath your ideas of who I should be.

I forgive you, ex-love-of-my-life,
for not seeing who I've become
beneath your visions of who I used to be.

I forgive you, ex-partner,
for not seeing who I've always been
beneath the farce I kept feeding you of who I was.

I forgive you, lover,
for not hearing my body
beneath the drone of trauma I didn't heal or explain.

I forgive you, muse,
for being unable to surface for words from
beneath the tsunamis of poems I had to become.

I forgive you, authority figure who tries to control me
for not seeing the importance of my autonomy
beneath your phobia of it.

I forgive you, male stranger who interrupts me
while I'm writing or dancing or thinking,
for not acknowledging my stream of consciousness
beneath your fantasies about my body.

I forgive you all for me,
for all the creative potential entombed
beneath stifled spite and washed down words.

—If this is not forgiveness, I don't want it.

EYE OPEN

Spirituality is not a cure
for anger, sadness, grief,
pain, doubt, suffering.

It is an invitation:
come into the house
of sorrows. Stay. Feel.

Look down the barrel.
Do not run.

Hold hands with loss.
Do not turn away.

Keep your eyes
locked with the gaze
of the flaming abyss.

Learn to love it all.
Earn your birthright
to love it all.

WELCOME BACK. SORRY. PLEASE STAY.

It's not a party. It's a reunion. All my formerly exiled atoms have returned. Everyone is excited, annoyed, and on the verge of a fight (but at least they all showed up). I navigate strained small talk with those who slunk in the door dressed in reproof. *Nice of you to invite us all here now that he's gone*, they say. The angriest ones compare scars in the corner, complain loudly enough for me to overhear. *Yes, she was the one who built the iron curtain. Yes, she was the one who doped us and dragged us out by the ankles. Yes, she thinks it's all magically going to be okay now.* I join in, reveal my track marks, commiserate. They take off their coats, ask where the closet is (not to mistake it for a bedroom). Everyone is suspicious of the food, afraid I've poisoned it again, and I am the lunatic at my own reunion. But fervour by tremor, we mourn together. Keyhole by hatchet, we locate the punchlines. I have a lot to apologize for, but everyone seems willing to forgive. They crack jokes about the food but eat it anyway. In the dead air, it's not awkward. It's not painless. It's empty and lawless, but this is my family. This is my homecoming. This is my rebirth.

IF YOU FIND A TIME MACHINE, SEND THIS TO ME IN MARCH 2009

Dear you, I mean me,
it's the year 2020.

I know you think you're dying
preparing for your last days,
saying goodbye to those around you
by pushing them all away.

But... spoiler... you choose to stay.
Now, I'm living with the aftertaste
of all the help you wouldn't eat
so it rotted into screams to leave.

I forgive you for what you're about to do,
but all these years later, she still doesn't.
Stop running, take a moment.
Stop numbing, start being honest.

Please spend time sober and alone,
and when it feels wrong, trust.
Please Google "trauma bonding,"
and stop confusing love with lust.

Believe in the time machine magic of poetry.
We've got a date with who we are in 2023.
Hold on, baby. Do you hear me?
You're going to be okay. Believe.

Keep writing. Sing. Dance.
And please get some sleep.

NOTE TO SELF #17

Do not confuse happiness
with toxic positivity.

Do not confuse being conscious
with acting conscious.

Do not confuse the end of a word
with the end of a sentence.

Do not confuse healing
with censorship.

Do not confuse compassion
with codependency.

Do not confuse the end of a sentence
with the end of a chapter.

Do not confuse faith in the future
with fear of the present.

Do not confuse an opportunity
with a distraction.

Do not confuse the end of a chapter
with the end of the story.

Do not confuse forgiveness
with bottling anger.

Do not confuse inner peace
with ignorance.

Do not confuse the end of the story
with the end of the work.

TO THE "HEALER" WHO ASSAULTED ME

I'm not calling the police.

You don't deserve the respect
cops give men like you
in situations like these.

I'll handle you myself.

If I hear your name again—
offering my friends your "services,"
passing off violations as cures,
adding survivors on social media,
hunting for victims—

remember:
I know where you live.

I am not the prey you once met,
and I will make sure that
you never touch anyone
ever again.

Give me an excuse. I dare you.

This is your only and final
warning.

EVERY TRAGEDY NEEDS A POET

You don't know poetry
until you witness death:
how the gasps fade slowly,
how battle churns to peace.

You don't know poetry
until you shovel a grave:
how digging it takes muscle,
how filling it takes guts.

You don't know poetry
until you hear the silence:
how it is never absolute,
how loudly the wind breathes.

FENTANYL FAÇADE

We are going to funerals more often now,
she says, shows me the photo. Oh. Yes,
I knew him: another character killed off
to move the plot forward.

When will these kids learn to abstain,
they say, roll their eyes. No. No,
I don't agree: what's that powder in your
policies? Where does the tragedy begin?

CRUELTY-FREE MCFREEDOM

The Empaths are "clearing dark energy."
Will these herbs help remove the terror?
Flaunt your fair-trade elephant pants,
fall for fundamental attribution error.

Bypass, be kind, and quiet your mind,
buy baking soda deodorant, detox your soul.
Will these chakra crystals block bullets?
"Choose your reality. You're in control."

Enlightenment in four easy payments.
Will these affirmations fix inequality?
Connect to source and chant Kumbaya.
But why why "why do I feel so empty?"

SLICE

1.
I'm licking the razor edge again
but there was never any honey.
There's nothing on the blade.
It's in the blood, all of it.
When the minerals enter you,
what stings: sugar or salt?
It's not a chicken-egg thing.
Lick and lick and you'll know.

2.
I didn't see their tongues,
I used mine to call them my friends.
When I opened my mouth,
crying, bleeding, they blinked,
opened parted their lips,
caverns milky with scar tissue—
if there is one thing I am not,
it's someone who looks away.

3.
When it stains our teeth,
we both stop smiling for a while,
but I can throw this blade away,
go back to licking spoons.
My mother is shocked by it:
what's grown under my lips.
Your mother always knew,
and so did you. It's not fair.

OVERHEARD IN 2020

I worry about being blamed shot

It's not fun getting called out assaulted

Why can't people suck it up listen

How can you be so negative say nothing

I am so sick of this virus oppression

Can't we all just get along be left alone

Better check your tone of voice privilege

Was that enough of an apology proof

I can't breathe in this mask mama, please

Why can't you stop being dramatic interrupting

I didn't mean to offend you

Why is everything so political

Are you ignoring me

What did I do wrong

IT'S NOT OVER TILL
THE FAT PAYCHEQUE STINGS

They steal the joy in your mirror time,
sell it back to you for a few bucks.
You buy it in bulk, stock up for the year,
wonder why it doesn't work for you
like it does for the billboards.

SELF ACTUALIZATION
IN THE SECURE SECTION

The universe is in your favour,
ask and you will surely receive.
Never mind your privilege.
You always get what you need.

It's time to trust a higher power,
breathe deep and kill your ego.
Never mind those politics.
You are safe wherever you go.

Never mind the screams.
Succeed.
Never mind the smoke.
Believe.

STOP SNACKING ON SELF-DELUSION

If your soul feels heavy,
stop eating candied lies.
Ignorance is poisonous,
honeyed toxins inside.

Choose the unsweetened facts
over saccharine words.
When truth tastes too bitter,
don't spit it out, add some herbs.

Swallow those rank conflicts.
Drink up. Have one more round.
This is how you finally lose
all that's weighing you down.

NOTE TO SELF #18

Your feelings are valid
(and people who say they're not
won't help you express them).

Your mistakes are forgivable
(and people who say they're not
won't help you learn from them).

Your behaviours are malleable
(and people who say they're not
won't help you change them).

Your dreams are possible
(and people who say they're not
won't help you achieve them).

RED FEATHER

She said,
"I am rhetorical until further notice."

And I knew the madness was fire,
and she was the goddess Kali,
and I was there to learn patience.

She said,
"I scare people just by being myself."

And I knew the madness was a root,
and she was the center of the Sun,
and I was there to learn gratitude.

She is a medicine woman,
a cowgirl, and a mad scientist
in a love affair with the eternal.

They call her bipolar.
I call her Red Feather.

But when her art speaks, I am silent.
I am struck with the blinding truth,
and I am there to worship.

GUITAR GOD

(Elegy for Memphis Deville)

A blues enigma perched on a crate in the Annex,
cut-off gloves, dangling cigarette, parched lips,
a legend in dirty jeans and an oversized coat.

The only change he asked for was police reform.
With a glare like cement and words like plaster,
Stevie Ray Vaughan's soul visited Bloor and Bathurst.

Snow falls on long grey hair, streetlights sparkle,
hardened fingertips slide over a pastel Washburn.
Photos suspend time, ageless, endless oblivion.

I first saw the drawings at the funeral.
"None of us knew," his best friend said, eyes wide.
"I knew him forty years and didn't know him at all."

The church took cash donations for the art
while his friends curled their lips, shook their heads,
didn't wonder what he'd say about that.

It isn't that I don't know death is coming
for us all, and maybe it is naïve, but I never
meant it when I told him, "Goodbye."

Memphis taught me that tomorrow is an assumption.
A month after I didn't know he died, I saw him.
I saw him and didn't cross the street to say, "Hello."

THE GIRL WITH THE PINK UKULELE

The bible is a poetry book.
Turning water into wine:

his presence made people
giddy, honest, friendly, brave,

but there was only
water in their cups.

That's what you do.

The messiah has returned,
and she has your smile.

NO ONE

No one told us the sun was coming back.

We poured bleach in our eyes
and screamed for April.

No one told us when hide and seek was over.

We peeked from around the wall,
but everybody had already gone inside.

No one told us that skin stretches.

We cut ourselves open
to make room for growing backbones,
stuck roses we thieved from the neighbours
into windswept flesh.

No one told us the flowers were blooming,
wilting,
decaying.

We saw it already of course
but we had learned to assume
we were imagining things.

No one told us the wounds were healing.

We confused scars with infections
and infections with bandages.
We murdered our regenerated cells
and praised the glory of gangrene.

No one told us we deserved thin skin,
sacred sin,
time.

We took shots of tar every night,
drank antifreeze every weekend,
swallowed mercury once a month.

No one offered us water.

NO ONE offered us water.

We burned our buzz cuts in the desert sun,
burned our fingerprints on our boot buckles,
burned our underpants just to smell the smoke.

No one took away our matches
after we doused ourselves in gasoline.

We screamed, but we never died;
even when we died, we kept on living.

No one knew what to say at our funerals.

We haunted each other in strife and health.
We loved ghosts more than we loved people
because we knew how to be disturbed
and we knew how to love thin air.

No one taught us how to stay.

No one figured out how to make us stay.

No one loved us enough to make us want to stay.

We earned honorary degrees in departure:
a language we invented and sold
to those who never arrived like we did.

No one told us it was beautiful, the wreckage.

We stopped trying to clean it up,
threw Molotov cocktails at piles of Past,
entire civilizations trapped inside.

No one told us it wasn't our fault.

We wouldn't believe that anyway.

No one told us it wasn't our fault.

But we don't believe in blame.

No one told us it wasn't our fault.

We heard children shrieking, climbed
under, got bloodstains on our cheeks,
emerged with one terrified infant
old enough to weep for its parents.

No one told us it was a metaphor.

We spent all our money on diapers,
came home to a teenager with a sour face
saying this wasn't the kind of shit
we were going to be cleaning up today.

No one told us it was a metaphor.

We made an extra set of keys.

No one told us it was a metaphor.

When the sheriff came to examine
the fumes and debris, we gave him
all our lighters. He gave us matches.

No one told us how to say No.

No One told us how to say NO.

We sang it.

No One harmonized.

We loved No One, that faithful friend.

And No One? No One loved us back.

NEW MESSAGE FROM YOU KNOW WHO

I made you how I made you.
You ask for my help
but mistrust my design?

Every time you wonder
if you're good enough,
you're questioning me.

Doubt me all you want,
but don't beg me for
what I already gave you.

Find it inside yourself.

DOUBLE-EDGED WORDS

The more I listen,
the more I speak.

What a spoiled brat:
expecting tenderness
wherever, whenever.

The more I give,
the more I want.

This must be why
I abandoned myself
in the first place.

The more I try,
the more I expect.

What a burden:
parenting a child
who never grows up.

The more I care,
the more I need.

I'm tired but
I'm not leaving.

I'm not walking
out on myself
anymore.

GRANDPA WAS A NAGAYBAK. SO AM I.

(In memory of Misha Tugalyev 1938 - 2020)

I never knew these things. I mean, who even knew Russia had indigenous people? Did you? I didn't. My grandmother says my family in Kzil Yelga would love to meet me. I can't even pronounce it properly. What would they think of my English accent? Could I learn Tatar? It's not about language. It's about history. Ukrainzi. Tatari. Nagaybaki. I have roots. Why did it take a funeral for me to want to touch them? It's not about geography. There's a thread. It ties everything too tightly. I see the seeds that formed the branches woven into veniki that long lashed my cheeks. It's not about forgiveness. It's about all the conversations I can never have now that I have questions to ask. It's not about death. It's about the way life drones on casually while the deeper things stay packed in boxes. It's all the folk songs I'll never learn. It's the way my roots are dangling from my feet. It's about time. It's about time and the way it never stops.

NOTE TO SELF #19

Live each day
as if you've already
been guaranteed
everything you want,
and you're on your way
to pick it up.

NEW MESSAGE FROM TOMORROW

You will get lost. You will bleed.
You will scream into the abyss
and hear nothing but an echo.

You will fall. You will bruise.
You will howl, look up at the rising moon,
and see the splendour of night.

You will sleep. You will dream.
You will wake up, look in the mirror,
and see galaxies in your eyes.

You will smile.
You will sing into the abyss
and dance to the echo.

You will smile.
You will smile,
and you will mean it.

NEW VOICEMAIL FROM THE FUTURE

Yes, we burned the bridge back to Normal.
It's okay, peer to the rock bottom of the canyon,
rage, weep, blame us, scream until you're sore,

take this time to say, "Goodbye."

But when you finally glance up at the monsters
stranded over there, pacing, blowing smoke,
when you finally grasp that you've been rescued,

don't forget to say, "Thank you."

10 COMMANDMENTS FOR THE NEW RAGE

1. Real healing opens all the doors and overturns all the furniture. Stop apologizing for the mess.

2. When your gut says No, don't pretend Yes.

3. Don't romanticize people's words. Don't assume their thoughts. Watch. What. They. Do.

4. Stop waiting for the right moment to leave, to change, to start. You can't avoid upsetting people. You don't owe anyone your consistency. You can't avoid the mistakes you need to make to become who you're meant to be.

5. A muse and a partner are two different things. Don't try to make one into the other. And don't let either one make you into someone you're not.

6. Some people will miss Tame Old You. Let them. Don't stop howling at the moon. Don't stop rooting into the dirt. Stay wild. Stay real. Stop justifying your freedom.

7. Protect your time. Protect your energy. No One is entitled to your attention or cooperation.

8. Learn the art of self. Self-examine. Self-care. Self-pleasure. Selfie your art. Stop waiting for someone else to capture your radiance.

9. Everything you want comes with everything you fear. Get ready to feel, baby. Get ready to grow. Get ready to show them who you are.

10. Find what makes you feel full and not just filled. Seek wholeness. There is no high like self-love.

GLOW

EPILOGUE

Everything is sorted. Everything has a place except the love poems I wrote to you. They are unclassified. I should burn them, I think. Or frame them. Or send them to you smeared in tears or blood or the juices of someone who deserves these words. But I don't know your address and that someone doesn't exist (yet). Besides, it's all a sideshow to accompany the main event: a ceremony. But what kind? Is it better to have fucked without love than never fucked at all? Is it better to have loved than blah blah? Sounds like New Age nonsense, but let's face it: I've always been a sucker for that stuff. I put a few poems in the last chapter: proof that I can still feel something so powerful after what I've lost. Is this the end? I'm still alone. You're still as emotionally unavailable as I will never admit I am. If you had loved me, it would have been different, but you didn't and I'm writing the epilogue of a story I never meant to tell. I've tried so hard to keep myself from being too much, loving too much, giving too much. But what is too much? Too much for whom? This is who I am. This *is* the end. This is a ceremony of surrender. This is a new kind of faith. I trust that my heart's capacity is not a freakish mistake. I trust that destiny is eager to dry my cheeks. Most of all, I trust that I will fall into poems again, and that someday, someone will fall deeply into poems with me.

ACKNOWLEDGMENTS

If you needed these words, I'm glad they found you.

If you're in these poems and still love me, thank you.
If you're in these poems and hurt me, I forgive you.

If you're in these poems and mad about it, sorry.
If you're not in these poems and mad about it, sorry?

If this makes you feel, it was for you.
If it makes you write, it was for you.

Mom, I love you.

God, damn. I mean, thanks.

ACKNOWLEDGMENTS 2

Megan Faith / Thabani Tshuma / David Silverberg / Andrea Thompson / Dwayne Morgan / Adrian Currie / Dylan Piercey / Yana Kolesnikova / Aiesha Bristol / Kath Lee-Jones / Christian Yamada / Anto Chan / Jemstone Masters / Tania Marcela Diaz Vasquez / Zarqui Edwards / Beki Bobrovski / Kelly McEvoy / Andi Stewart / Ivy Xantara / Malena S. Brooks

Toronto Poetry Slam / Up From the Roots / Poetryspective / Dead Poet / R.I.S.E Edutainment / Blank Canvas Gallery / Melbourne Spoken Word / Vancouver Poetry House / The Factory Honolulu / Slamalamadingdong

NW / JWR / Z / DS / AS

ABOUT THE AUTHOR

Vironika Wilde / Tugaleva / Nikulya / Viro / Nika

poet / feminist / nomad / vocalist / cat fanatic /
queer / immigrant / survivor / tree hugger / activist

crossing borders / gazing at the stars / pickles /
coffee / getting lost in the woods / questioning
authority / avocadoes / dancing in the rain

Instagram / Facebook / YouTube / vironika.org

NEW RELEASE: TOO MUCH FOR YOU

(Spoken word album)

A poetic journey that's seductive, heartbreaking, and refreshingly honest. Vironika Wilde's debut album of spoken word poems is an emotional rollercoaster through lust and love, doubt and faith, self-love and self-hatred. Bring your broken heart, grab a box of tissues, and get ready to revaluate the meaning of a happy ending.

Too Much for You is coming to Spotify and other streaming platforms on November 22, 2020.

BONUS

Q & A / THINGS PEOPLE ALWAYS ASK ME

Q: How long have you been writing?
A: Since I could hold a pen.

Q: Where do you get your inspiration?
A: Inspiration is a chemical reaction between my emotional landscape and my reality. It is unpredictable. After I finished *Deaf Republic* by Ilya Kaminsky, I wrote 17 poems in one day. But I couldn't have written them without the experiences they reference (e.g. my childhood memories or my conversations with my grandmother). Before I write, I often feel the weight of unsaid words, but I can't predict what will trigger this awareness or how heavy the words will be.

Q: Is it hard to be a poet nowadays?
A: I don't know if it's ever been easy to be a poet, but I would say it's easier now than ever. Poetry is making a comeback in this generation because it's closer to a TV show than a 600-page epic. People don't read as much as they used to. I'm not upset. It's a challenge to be more concise.

Q: What is your purpose as an artist?
A: My work is, primarily, internal. I must feel my own feelings, and I have a lot of them. After I'm honest with myself, I can be honest in my art. This honesty translates to liberation for those who need a dose of truth. My purpose is to make people feel the things they need to feel to move forward.

NOTES TO SELF #20-30

Fun fact: every Note to Self in this book is a real piece of me-to-me writing. Here are some that didn't make it into *Love and Gaslight* but held my hand through the storm nonetheless.

1. When you set boundaries out of self-love,
    some will call you insensitive.
    When you give out of generosity,
    some will call you manipulative.
    Someone will always misunderstand
    your presence in this world.
    Make sure it isn't you.

2. If you do not let yourself be seen,
    you cannot see.

3. Is it love or are you
    modernizing your trauma?
    Is it love or are you
    projecting your fantasies?
    Is it love or are you
    donating your power?
    Is it love or are you
    romanticizing dependency?

4. You are not a summary of your rehearsed poses.
    You are not a gently lifted eyebrow.
    You are not a coy, sideways smile.
    You are chaotic and, most importantly, real.

5. Sometimes, to love people,
    you must completely avoid them.
    Sometimes, to be strong,
    you must completely fall apart.

6. Don't let who you were yesterday keep you
   from becoming who you're meant to be today.

7. Stop sabotaging yourself by waiting for
   the perfect moment to begin. Nothing
   works perfectly the first time or the first
   fifty times. Everything has a learning curve.
   The beginning is just that—a beginning.
   Surrender your desire to do it flawlessly
   on the first try. It's not possible. Learn to learn.
   Learn to fail. Learn to learn from failing.
   And begin today. Begin now. Stop waiting.

8. To the people who drink your paragraphs
   but respond with emojis,
   to the people who borrow your time and money
   but never buy your art,
   to the people who dance in your passion
   but throw advice at your angst,
   to the people who eat your sweetest fruits
   but never water your roots,
   honey, you don't owe them
   a goddamned thing.

9. When you start to miss men from your past,
   remember all the bad sex you had with them.
   When you start fantasizing familiar fairy tales,
   remember how much bad sex could be involved.

10. The more attention you get,
    the more some people will be jealous of it
    and the more they will feel justified
    in talking about your life as something they
    understand and have opinions about.
    Embrace it. Don't feed the trolls.
    Walk headfirst into your daydreams
    and accept the garbage that comes
    with this size of a production.

ADVICE ON WRITING

I once started a podcast about writing. I cancelled it after one show because I didn't have enough to say. Here it all is.

1. Do not write for glory. Do not write for money or fame. Write *only* if you *must*.

2. Writing is a conversation. Are you making time and space for it? Are you listening? Are you opening up? Are you *genuinely* listening?

3. Don't judge your sources of inspiration. You don't know how it will all come together. Trust.

4. Done your draft? Rest for a few weeks. Edit it again. Read it out loud. Wait a month. Edit it again. Again. Edit until you're sick of editing. Edit some more. Take responsibility for your work.

5. You do not write poetry. You do not make art. You do not tell stories. Remember this. Art makes itself through you. Poetry writes itself through you. Stories tell themselves through you. Show some respect. Be an open channel. Say thank you. If it's not coming, don't blame the art form. Look in the mirror. Be nice. Don't lie.

6. Learn to laugh at trolls and hate mail.

7. Tell the truth. Use euphemisms and metaphors and abstractions, but tell the truth. As in, don't lie, but also don't omit the unsavoury chapters of your life. The parts you call ugly are the ones we all want to (and need to) see.

POETRY BOOKS I RECOMMEND

If you're a poet, I'd say read as many poetry books as possible, not only the "good" ones. The ones that repulse you can teach you more about writing than the ones that inspire you. That being said, here are some books that have inspired me:

★ Yrsa Daley-Ward - *Bone*

★ Andrea Gibson - *The Madness Vase*

★ Rudy Francisco - *Helium*

★ Danez Smith - *Black Movie*

★ Rupi Kaur - *The Sun and Her Flowers*

★ Olivia Gatwood - *Life of the Party*

★ Nayyirah Waheed - *salt.*

★ Ilya Kaminsky - *Deaf Republic*

★ Nikki Giovanni - *The Collected Poetry of Nikki Giovanni*

★ Andrea Gibson - *Lord of the Butterflies*

★ Randell Adjei - *I Am Not My Struggles*

★ Rachel Wiley - *Nothing is Okay*

★ Morgan Parker - *There Are More Beautiful Things Than Beyonce*

DID YOU LIKE IT?

...Did you?

Well, you must have.
You came all the way here.

Aw.

Babe.

I love you too.